AF473864

"Typefaces' full potential is not revealed until you've run the whole mac routine with it. Convert it to paths and mess it up, split it, slant it, stretch it, change the line width, funk it, spike it, remix it, rip it up, use it, abuse it, but most of all, have fun with it!"

— Cornel Windlin

Swiss type designer. He won the Jan Tschichold Prize in 1997 and founded the type foundry "Lineto" with his partners in 1998.

TD	Type Designer
TE	Type Engineer
F	Type Foundry
D	Designer
AD	Art/Design Director
CD	Creative Director
DA	Design Agency/Studio
CL	Client

I。What?

Bizarre typefaces take an unusual path by pushing the outer edge of the boundary and breaking the rules of design in different dimensions. They catch the eyes through visual disruption and identification interference. With stress on the deformation, distortion, dissolution and expansion of font form and structure, they underscore the tension and expressiveness of fonts as visual graphic shapes.Bizarre Typefaces included in this book are designed by independent or commercial type foundries, customized fonts designed for brands, and experimental fonts.

Typefaces embody the voice of language, has some neglected potentials other than its semantic function often neglected. For instance, the first san-serif was given the name “grotesque” due to its unusual weirdness, which has remained up to now.

With the development of the type design, such astonishment that came with san-serif may fall short of expressing the barriers that have been breached. Currently, the deformed fonts represent the image freely like dancers beyond the verbal dimension. Some type designers use exaggerated shapes topersonify fonts, while others challenge the visual recognition by compressing or distorting the fonts. Unsatisfied with the status quo, people have made various attempts to guide the type design to focus on the aesthetics from the single functionality. This book summarizes 8 universal font-variant techniques and 72 examples and encourages the readers to create their own bizarre typefaces matched with different techniques. Please keep in mind the quote on the title page:“ Typefaces’ full potential is not revealed until you’ve run the whole mac routine with it. Convert it to paths and mess it up, split it, slant it, stretch it, change the line width, funk it, spike it, remix it, rip it up, use it, abuse it, but most of all, have fun with it! ”

Any technique or rule is no more than a guide. Just break the rules and create your own font! We expect that this book would bring stirring inspiration to the type design in the complex context.

II 。**Ah! A→H**

Rule-based

Preset a System

As the most basic rule of type design, the Rule-based Approach has preset a set of scopes, boundaries, and norms for type design that allow designers to explore more possibilities for creation within certain tools, methods, or systems. Taking the grid system, the most representative tool in the Approach, as an example, the size and style of the grid should be determined in the first place. Among the system, the matts grid is the most basic design format. It would present the fonts with unique style by designing words within the unusual grid and adjusting the gradient or shape (isosceles triangle, rectangle diagonal, hexagon diagonal, etc.) of the conventional table cell. There are a lot of ideas to be found with the grid, some of which are beyond your imagination. In earlier human history, the moveable blocks used in the typography serve as grids in nature. Although the countless fonts are available, grids are always the best place to start for designers who would like to create personalized fonts.

The font *Hofmann* introduced later was drawn on the grid system established by the Swiss design master Hofmann in the 20th century, and explored another form of expression within the improved grids. There is another creation method in the scope of the approach, like *NRV*, with an attempt to break through all possibilities of type design by the use of limited tools.

Quote

"I might ignore the grid altogether after the first trails, buit it is always a good starting point. Grid is therefore nothing more than a starting point of someone else wanting to draw a typeface."

—Erik Spiekermann

"The grid is like the lines on a football field. You can play a great game in the grid or a lousy game. But the goal is to play a really fine game."

—Wim Crouwel

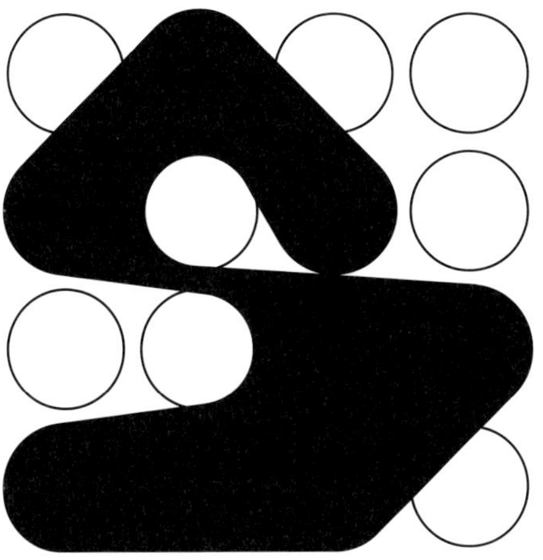

HOFMANN
P242

EARTHLAB SANS
P052

Conceptualization

Visual Simulation and Extension

Conceptualization is a technique to highly abstract the form and meaning of fonts. Designers integrate the specific lifestyles, social ethos or cultural issues into typefaces, the artistic symbols, in pursuit of the intrinsic uniformity of aesthetics and spirit by unifying form and meaning.

Coastline, one of the fonts included in the book, is a typographic design of conceptualization characterized by attaching a moral to the form. The designer takes the humanistic and environmental awareness as the original intention of the design, and abstracts the topographic features of glaciers submerged after melting to compose a set of fonts. The integration of concept and design is reflected in the grotesque font, with the purpose of alerting the society to the threat and destruction to the human society caused by global warming. The pairing of form and meaning functions as a voice. As for the Chinese font meaning Verbal Abuse, the designer leverages the abstract concepts of the trauma caused by the evil words of the parents to the hearts of children, to design the visual images in accordance with this concept. Inspired by individual states, emotions or social collective phenomena observed by the designers, these conceptualized works express emotional synaesthesia through the simulation and extension of the visual forms.

Quote

"Typographic abstraction only succeeds when there is an anchor in the real world. The look can be anarchic but its message should not be entirely obscured by an artistic impulse. Abstraction should be used as the hook that leads you to the information."

—— Steven Heller & Gail Anderson

BRASSIA
P226

COASTLINE
P296

Ornamentation

Jump Out of the Stereotype

Ornamentation, one of the effective methods to enhance the visual aesthetics of the fonts, would personify and endow the fonts with the expressiveness of space, lines and forms. The method includes three-dimensional processing and decoration. The former is a typical ornamentation, making the design “stereoscopic”, as if putting platform shoes on the fonts. Certainly, it is more suitable for the headings due to the eye-catching effect.

Transforming fonts into three-dimensional illusions in the layout of the graphic design is one of the ways designers interact with the readers by means of creating “false impression”. An impressive poster might be credited to the sincerity of the designer, or the subconscious illusion created by the poster. There is another method of ornamentation in addition to the three-dimensional processing. The computer-aided brushes or different materials on the scene could be used to create fonts. In the days of customized type design, a variety of fonts would be created by changing such variables as the brush, the orientation or the thickness. Just have a try and embrace unexpected discoveries and surprises.

Quote

“Think more about ideas and concepts than forms and that typography has now become a more ambivalent speciality, that both speaks to our minds and to our intellect because the shapes materialise ideas while also stimulating our emotions through their visual characteristics.”

——Morgane Vantorre

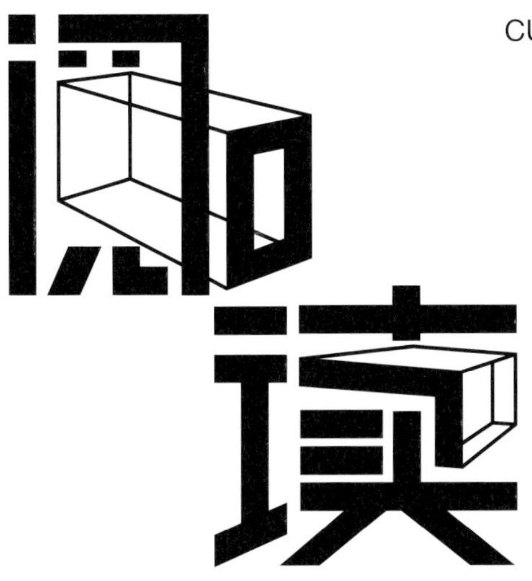

CUBIC TYPOGRAPHY
P140

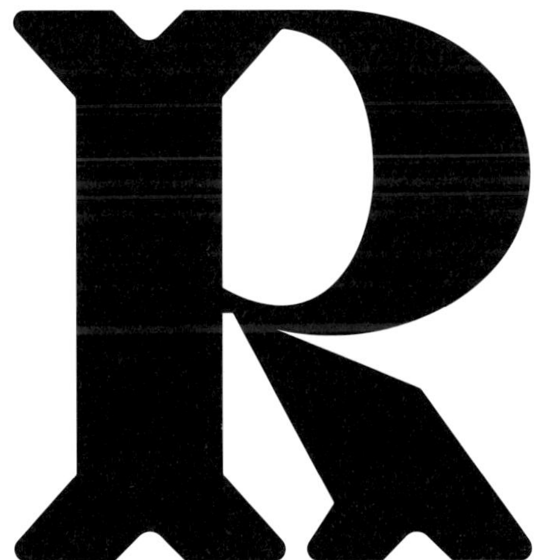

JAGER
P402

Graphication

Create the Visual Pun

It is easy to perceive the graphical technique in which the font is viewed as a part of visual element instead of merely an identifier. The relationship between fonts and graphics can be traced back to the early days, when all the oldest fonts, such as Egyptian hieroglyphs and Chinese oracle bone inscriptions, take graphics as the original typeface. Therefore, the characters and images were integrated at the very first, and gradually separated with the development of writing system. Now, the graphical thinking offers designers a new and broader perspective in terms of the type design. The pioneering graphic designer Neville Brody used to be averse to the type design, but later found, from the new perspective, that it wasn't conventional any more.

Afterwards, the type design inclines to be more expressive and visually diverse style by breaking free from the subordinating and utilitarian role of recognizability. The graphics of fonts, inspired by the concrete, daily and touchable objects, simulate the visual design in the artistic form, temperament and spirit to some extent. The fonts are endowed with a new role of graphical medium of information, bringing visual feast which lies between functional property and ornamental value.

Quote

"The future of typography is about beauty and humanity, with the ultimate goal of expressing feeling."

——itsnicethat.com

"What we call pictorial type may not be pure typography, but it can be effective design."

——The Typography Idea Book

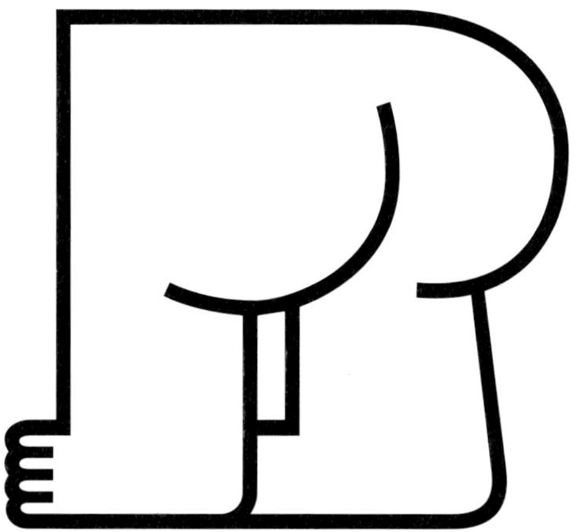

TYPEFESSE
P066

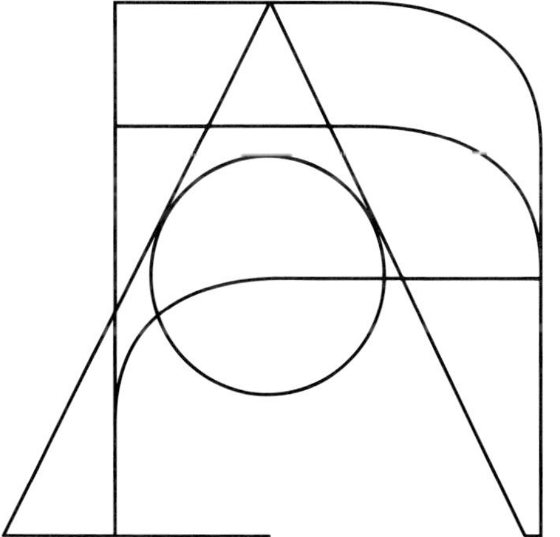

SCREEN SPLASH
P202

Digitalization

Take a Single Pixel as Tool

Digitalization specifically refers to the techniques used in the design of bitmap fonts with the pixel style. The fonts reveal the pure vitality of the early cyber-space even in the high-resolution era, and now serve as the symbol of visual culture in a specific era. The 8×8 mono-spaced bitmap font is regarded as the most common format in the world of games. The design of bitmap fonts, like building LEGO blocks, is required to piece the glyphs together by filling pixels one by one in the bottom-up approach. All bitmap fonts are composed of curved and straight lines.

It is the glyphs "B" "E" and "S", as well as the numbers "2""3""5" and "6" that challenge the designers the most in the above process. *Dinkie Bitmap*, a representative Chinese bitmap font included in the book, pushes the envelope of the minimum pixel size, and creates a multilingual bitmap font family with high legibility. Pixel is the smallest unit of color block on the screen. The word "pixel" is a coinage which compounds "picture" and "element". The typeface created by digital graphics features the characteristics of the times, regardless of trivial matters.

Quote

"Bitmap letterforms are the runic letters of our times. In the future we will look at these characters and wonder why there was ever a need for making such primitive and illegible type."

——Just van Rossum

MONDWEST & NEUEBIT TYPEFACES

P094

¶AaBbCc

→12345

Pangram²

CA—CE

DINKIE BITMAP

P108

铁道 ← 铁道

Re-creation

Stand on the Shoulders of Giants

Re-creation is a technique that takes the existing fonts as the basis and draws inspiration from them, starting with choosing a set of font that would keep on developing. The first step is to take a close look at the basic fonts, followed by clarifying the direction for further design. The purpose of re-creation is to adapt, extend and expand the meanings of existing fonts, and break and cross boundaries. The unique features are required to be created so as to draw public concern.

In the project Point, Line, and Shape shown in the following sections, the new font *Ming Romantic*™ was designed with the *Songti* as prototype, the font on the book cover of *The Bell Jar* was designed based on the font *Lora*, and the Chinese font *The Violence of Language* was re-created on the basis of *Regular Script*, all of which reflect the essence of this technique. The original font, regarded as graphic element, is greatly stretched and deformed without considering its practicability, and integrated with media and ideas to enhance the intrinsic features. The font is endowed with emotions and stories to present a new form.

Quote

"I believe that to be heard, you have to make a little noise, noise whose frequencies move beyond the normal wavelengths.The noise may be cacophony to some - just as John Coltrane's saxophone might once have sounded - so bit it."

—— Paul Sych

THE VIOLENCE OF LANGUAGE
P104

To the person
in the bell jar,
blank and stopped
as a dead baby,
the world itself
is a bad dream.

ESTHER
P302

Combination

Deconstruction and Collage of Graphics

Combination Method, a technique that can be commonly used in multiple fonts, is composed of two forms. The former is the random combination of fonts, such as the technique Torn Letter invented by Alan Fletch who is the former partner of the Pentagram. Currently the technique is more officially named "Sampling". The creation of collage with strong randomness expresses the symbiosis of various fonts, in which the flexible characteristic of language is visualized. It makes use of recombination, pairing and collage to process the elements of various fonts fully or partially divided into. For example, by selecting and recombining the seemingly recycled letters in distinctive styles from the fonts in magazines, an invisible rhythm would surprisingly come into being as visual-lingual symbols.

The latter technique focuses on the type design itself, where the structural elements that make up a typeface are viewed as independent design elements. They are recombined to develop a new typeface , i.e., the Modular Typeface. It is formed by pre-designed structural elements that are repeatedly used to develop a set of fonts. The Modular Typeface has quite distinctive feature of collage, in the coherent and unified style full of interest and creativity.

Quote *"Words have meaning. Type has spirit. The combination is spectacular."*

—— Paula Scher

KREIS
P172

RESPIRA BLACK
P338

Respira
Black

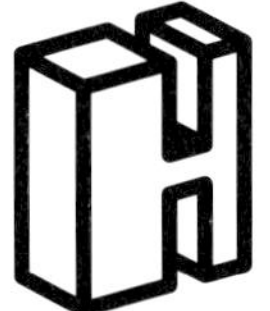

Exaggeration

Beyond the Typeface Itself

Exaggeration is a technique that gives rise to the typeface with sharp contrast and distinctive style by highlighting specific parts. Exaggeration is always accompanied with contrast, for which *NRV* is a good example. The designer deliberately lengthens the lower part of the fonts, each of which is like walking on stilts, to move upwards the center of gravity. The narrow counter and small opening present a sharp contrast. With much room to play, exaggeration can be used to create fonts with unique styles by highlighting the contrast between the weight or the stem and the horizontal strokes, condensing and extending the proportion of the font and negative space dynamically, or magnifying the features of different styles and recombining them. The method endows the font with ornamental value and expressiveness of visual graphics, which brings visual impact and shows the tension of symbol art.

Apart from the spatial contrast from within, visual coherence is required to be retained. The technique is more than just highlighting, extending or condensing. The relationship between the elements and the balance between the elements are the whole matter as well.

Quote

"A typeface is a new body for a voice long out of its speaker's body, committed to words but indifferent to the language of words, and further estranged from the language of voice."

——Paul Elliman

"Readability is a conditioned state, I wanted to take the role of typography away from a purely subservient, practical role towards one that is potentially more expressive and visually dynamic."

——Neville Brody

NRV
P076

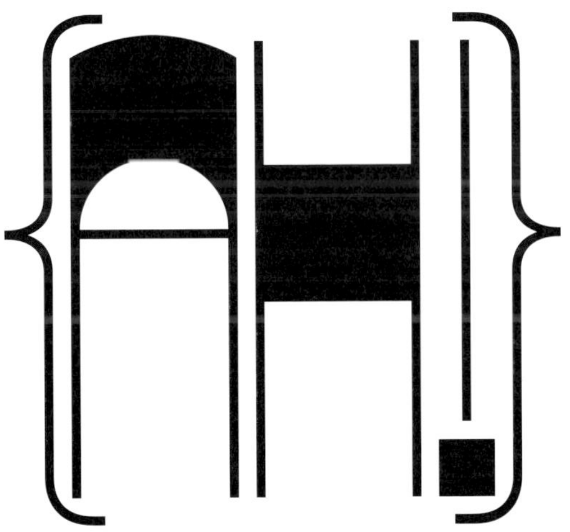

ZOO
P264

▯▯▯。WOW!deas

 Rule-based

 Conceptualization

 Ornamentation

Graphication

 Digitalization

 Re-creation

 Combination

Exaggeration

Part 1.
BEHIND THE TYPE

Thinking & Process

BROKAT V-1.0 BY BOAFFF

01. BROKAT

Designers at the Hugmun Studio, commissioned by Cinemateket Trondheim, an arthouse cinema , designed a set of grotesque posters for the cinema's monthly program.

The font *Brokat*, which stands for "shining" in Polish, was designed with the visual symbolism of the stars. By using thick serifs and thin horizontal lines, it visually echos with the traditional fonts in old Western movies.

TD: Maria Milenko. Tomasz Pawluk
DA: Hugmun Studio

A Á Â

Ä À Ā

Ą Å Ã

1 2 3

4 5 6

7 8 9

DĄB

SØR

MIST

QUIZ!

DRAX

Juli
August
cinemateket
sommer
ferie
BILLETTSALG PÅ
CINEMATEKET-TRONDHEIM.NO
bar Ingmar
TRONDHEIM KOMMUNE
Norsk filminstitutt

NOVEMBER & DESEMBER

cinemateket

Fre 01.11 kl 18.00 **Push** | Fredrik Gertten - Sverige 2019 - 1t 32m
Søn 03.11 kl 18.00 **A Dog Called Money** | Seamus Murphy - Irland 2019 - 1t 34m
Søn 03.11 kl 20.00 **Barn** | Dag Johan Haugerud - Norge 2019 - 2t 37m
Ons 06.11 kl 18.30 **A Dog Called Money** | Seamus Murphy - Irland 2019 - 1t 34m
Ons 06.11 kl 20.30 **Gåten Kaspar Hauser** | Werner Herzog - Vest-Tyskland 1974 - 1t 50m
Tors 07.11 kl 18.00 **Fight Club** | David Fincher - USA 1999 - 2t 19m
Tors 07.11 kl 20.45 **Push** | Fredrik Gertten - Sverige 2019 - 1t 32m
Fre 08.11 kl 18.00 **Uår** | Julie Lunde Lillesæter - Norge 2019 - 28m
Vises i samarbeid med Utviklingsfondet og Spire Trondheim. Gratis inngang!
Fre 08.11 kl 20.00 Syriske Filmdager i Trondheim: **Another News Story** | Orban Wallace - Storbritannina 2018 - 1t 25m
Forfilm: **Soulala** - 10m
Lør 09.11 kl 14.00 Barnefilmklubben: **Whisper of the Heart** | Yoshifumi Kondō - Japan 1995 - 1t 51m
Lør 09.11 kl 18.30 Syriske Filmdager i Trondheim: | **The Borrowed Dress** | Leen Alfaisal - Syria 2018 - 54m
Søn 10.11 kl 18.00 **Gåten Kaspar Hauser** | Werner Herzog - Vest-Tyskland 1974 - 1t 50m
Søn 10.11 kl 20.15 **Fight Club** | David Fincher - USA 1999 - 2t 19m
Ons 13.11 kl 18.00 Trondheim Filmklubb: **The Camino Voyage** | Donal O'Ceilleachair - Irland 2018 - 1t 37m
Ons 13.11 kl 20.00 **Fight Club** | David Fincher - USA 1999 - 2t 19m
Tors 14.11 kl 18.00 Miljøfilm: **Skogen verden glemte** | Ulf Myrvold - Norge 2012 - 58m
Vises i samarbeid med Naturvernforbundet i Trøndelag. Gratis inngang!
Tors 14.11 kl 20.00 **High Life** | Claire Denis - Storbritannia/Frankrike 2018 - 1t 53m
Fre 15.11 kl 18.00 **High Life** | Claire Denis - Storbritannia/Frankrike 2018 - 1t 53m
Fre 15.11 kl 20.30 **White Material** | Claire Denis - Frankrike/Kamerun 2009 - 1t 42m
Søn 17.11 kl 18.00 Trondheim Dokumentarfestival: **Trøndersk dokumentarfilm: Off the Grid / Togrevere / Arven / Balanse**
Regi: Vegard Dahle / Martin A. Walther / Mari Nilsen Neira / Marte Hallem
Søn 17.11 kl 20.00 **Barn** | Dag Johan Haugerud - Norge 2019 - 2t 37m
Ons 20.11 kl 18.00 Trondheim Filmklubb: **Madeline's Madeline** | Josephine Decker - USA 2018 - 1t 33m
Ons 20.11 kl 20.00 **High Life** | Claire Denis - Storbritannia/Frankrike 2018 - 1t 53m
Tors 21.11 kl 18.00 **White Material** | Claire Denis - Frankrike/Kamerun 2009 - 1t 42m
Tors 21.11 kl 20.00 **Early Spring** | Yasujirō Ozu - Japan 1956 - 2t 25m
Fre 22.11 kl 18.00 **The Irishman** | Martin Scorsese - USA 2019 - 3t 29m
Lør 23.11 kl 14.00 Barnefilmklubben: **Mulan** | Tony Bancroft, Barry Cook - USA 1998 - 1t 28m
Lør 23.11 kl 16.00 **The Irishman** | Martin Scorsese - USA 2019 - 3t 29m
Søn 24.11 kl 16.00 **The Irishman** | Martin Scorsese - USA 2019 - 3t 29m
Søn 24.11 kl 20.00 **Early Spring** | Yasujirō Ozu - Japan 1956 - 2t 25m
Tirs 26.11 kl 19.00 **The Irishman** | Martin Scorsese - USA 2019 - 3t 29m
Ons 27.11 kl 19.00 **The Irishman** | Martin Scorsese - USA 2019 - 3t 29m
Tors 28.11 kl 18.00 **Early Spring** | Yasujirō Ozu - Japan 1956 - 2t 25m
Tors 28.11 kl 20.45 **Bram Stoker's Dracula** | Francis Ford Coppola - USA 1992 - 2t 8m
Fre 29.11 kl 18.00 **Marriage Story** | Noah Baumbach - USA 2019 - 2t 16m
Fre 29.11 kl 20.45 **Bram Stoker's Dracula** | Francis Ford Coppola - USA 1992 - 2t 8m
Lør 30.11 kl 15.00 **Marriage Story** | Noah Baumbach - USA 2019 - 2t 16m
Søn 01.12 kl 16.00 **The Irishman** | Martin Scorsese - USA 2019 - 3t 29m
Søn 01.12 kl 20.00 **Marriage Story** | Noah Baumbach - USA 2019 - 2t 16m
Ons 04.12 kl 18.00 **Marriage Story** | Noah Baumbach - USA 2019 - 2t 16m
Ons 04.12 kl 20.45 **Bram Stoker's Dracula** | Francis Ford Coppola - USA 1992 - 2t 8m
Tors 05.12 kl 18.00 **Echo** | Rúnar Rúnarsson - Island 2019 - 1t 19m | Møt regissøren!
Tors 05.12 kl 20.45 **Ildfjell** | Rúnar Rúnarsson - Island 2011 - 1t 39m
Forfilm: **The Last Farm** | Rúnar Rúnarsson - Island 2004 - 15m
Søn 08.12 kl 18.00 **Småfugler** | Rúnar Rúnarsson - Island 2015 - 1t 39m
Søn 08.12 kl 20.30 **Echo** | Rúnar Rúnarsson - Island 2019 - 1t 19m
Ons 11.12 kl 18.00 **Ildfjell** | Rúnar Rúnarsson - Island 2011 - 1t 39m
Ons 11.12 kl 20.00 **Småfugler** | Rúnar Rúnarsson - Island 2015 - 1t 39m
Tors 12.12 kl 18.00 **Echo** | Rúnar Rúnarsson - Island 2019 - 1t 19m
Tors 12.12 kl 20.00 **It's a Wonderful Life** | Frank Capra - USA 1946 - 2t 10m
Fre 13.12 kl 18.00 **It's a Wonderful Life** | Frank Capra - USA 1946 - 2t 10m
Fre 13.12 kl 20.30 **The Two Popes** | Fernando Meirelles - Storbritannia 2019 - 2t 5m
Lør 14.12 kl 14.00 Barnefilmklubben: **Karsten og Petras vidunderlige jul** | Arne Lindtner Næss - Norge 2015 - 1t 15m
Søn 15.12 kl 18.00 **It's a Wonderful Life** | Frank Capra - USA 1946 - 2t 10m
Søn 15.12 kl 20.30 **The Two Popes** | Fernando Meirelles - Storbritannia 2019 - 2t 5m

BILLETTSALG PÅ
CINEMATEKET-TRONDHEIM.NO

bar Ingmar

TRONDHEIM KOMMUNE

Trøndelag fylkeskommune

Norsk filminstitutt

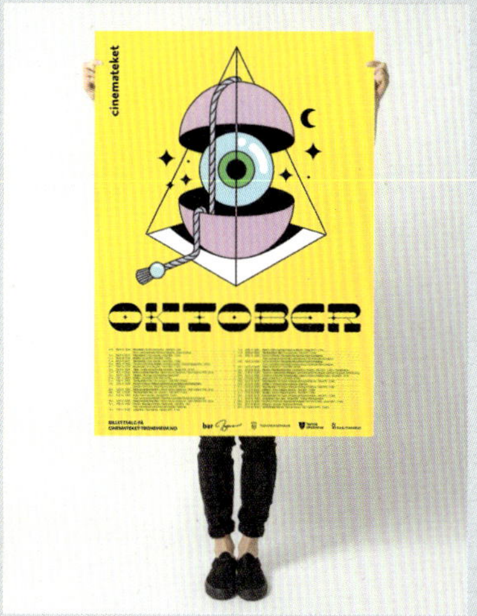

CL: Cinemateket Trondheim, Norway

The designers at Hugmun make a habit of skimming through their favorite but usually niche fonts little known to the public, to select from for their designs. As for this project, they believe that the type design is not only for information spreading, but also to reveal the character and style of the cinema. The use of unexpected fonts is the creative selling point.

They held that the chosen fonts are required to constitute the whole harmoniously, while creating a mysterious and lively visual world. Each font should have a style of its own and complement the illustrations. For example, designers use bold, dramatic and eye-catching fonts to highlight the headline messages, and prefer highly readable fonts to present the rich program contents.

Each poster is unique, and the constant tests and adjustments have to be made to create a good balance. They would start with a grid, and are dedicated to present a work with personal touch instead of sticking too precisely to the grid itself.

* The font *Brokat* was used only for the poster of October, as each monthly poster had its own typefaces individually designed. *Brokat* is also an open source font which is used by designers all over the world in various works and has received positive responses.

cinemateket
BILLETTSALG PÅ CINEMATEKET-TRONDHEIM.NO
Norsk filminstitutt
cinemateket
BILLETTSALG PÅ CINEMATEKET-TRONDHEIM.NO
cinemateket
JUNI
cinemateket
ril

BILLETTSALG PÅ
CINEMATEKET-TRONDHEIM.NO
Januar
Februar
OKTOBER
bar
TRONDHEIM KOMMUNE
Norsk filminstitutt
BILLETTSALG PÅ
CINEMATEKET-TRONDHEIM.NO
cinemateket
NOVEMBER & DESEMBER
LG PÅ CINEMATEKET-TRONDHEIM.NO
TRONDHEIM KOMMUNE
Norsk filminstitutt
teket

02. SKAC DISPLAY

Storm King Art Center Visual Design

The visual design project consists of the main icon and the original font *SKAC Display* designed specifically for the park area. By integrating the characteristics of the various sculptures of the art museum in the font, the designer creates contrasting strokes and negative spaces that highlight the abstract style and echo the features of the sculpture art. The font itself serves as grid of the layout to keep a sense of order.

TD: Tianqing Li
CL: Storm King Art Center

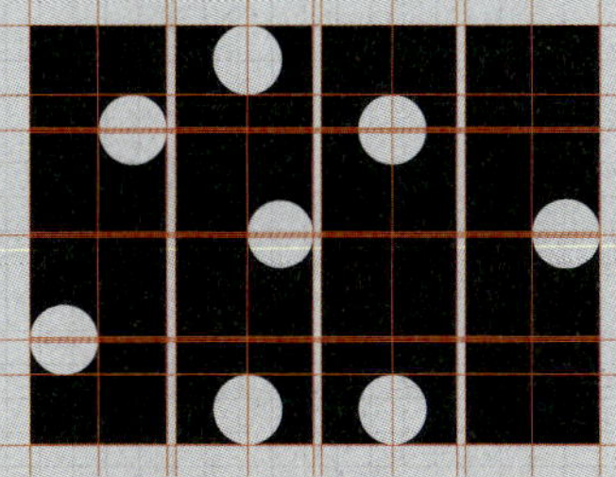

The Storm King Art Center (SKAC) is an open art gallery with outdoor landscape of broad view. It has a major collection of large outdoor contemporary sculptures, ranking first in the number of collections in the United States. The unique style has inspired the designer, who expects to create a timeless logo style based on the two main features of the gallery. While keeping the classic framing system simple and neat, the flexibility of the logo design highlights its richness and extensiveness, which echoes the characteristics of the geographical location.

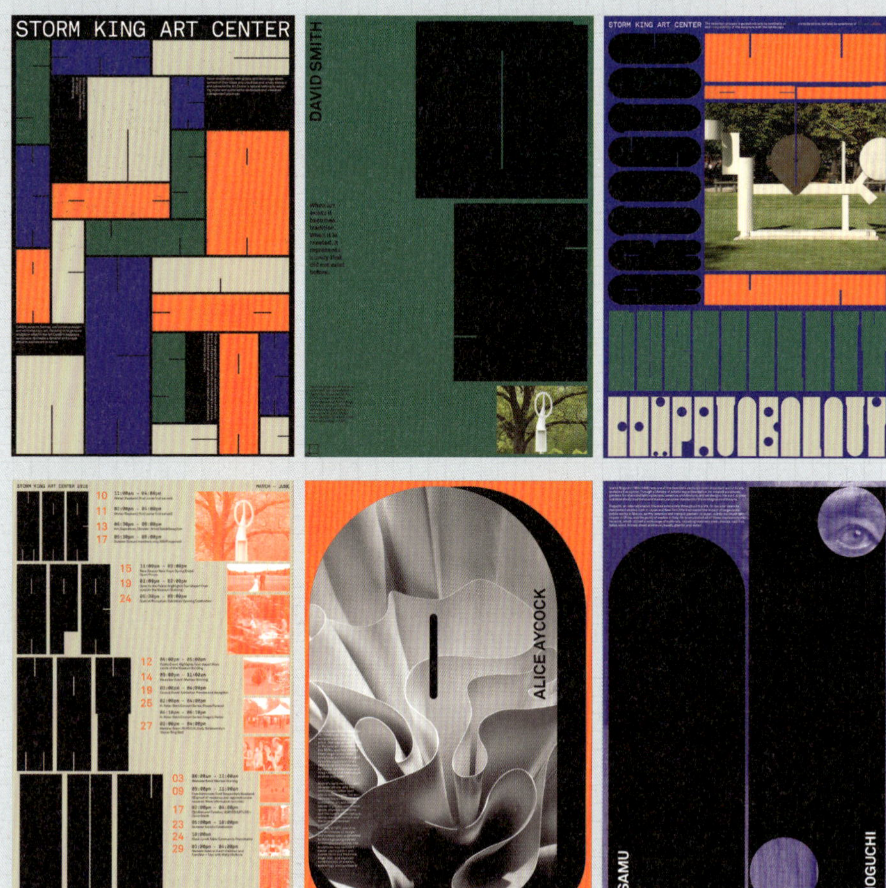
STORM KING ART CENTER
DAVID SMITH
STORM KING ART CENTER
ALICE AYCOCK
ISAMU
NOGUCHI

STORM KING ART CENTER

03. TAPETYPE

CalArts Graphic Design Program Show

The designer believes that choosing the proper font that reflects the style of the overall design is crucial to the final version. Therefore, the designer takes the image of tape to create *Tapetype* to highlight the theme of the CalArts Graphic Design Program Show.

TD: Junki Hong
CL: CalArts

ABCDEF
GHIJKLMN
OPQRSTU
VWXYZ

TAPE TYPE

The font is made up of horizontal and vertical strokes and 45-degree strokes. The strokes with the same thickness are overlapped to show the breadth of spirit. The designer highlights the overlap with the use of two colors of tape.

CALARTS
GRAPHIC DESIGN
PROGRAM
SHOW 2018
OPENING
MAY 3,
2018
7PM–
10PM
WORKS
IN
PRO-
GRESS
OPEN
MAY
4–10,
2018
11AM–
7PM
DAILY
MFA
D300
BFA
D301

calartsgd2018.com
WORKS IN PROGRESS
MFA
CALARTS
GRAPHIC DESIGN PROGRAM
SHOW 2018

calartsgd2018.com
WORKS IN PROGRESS
BFA
CALARTS
GRAPHIC DESIGN PROGRAM
SHOW 2018

WORKS
IN
PROGRESS

CALARTS

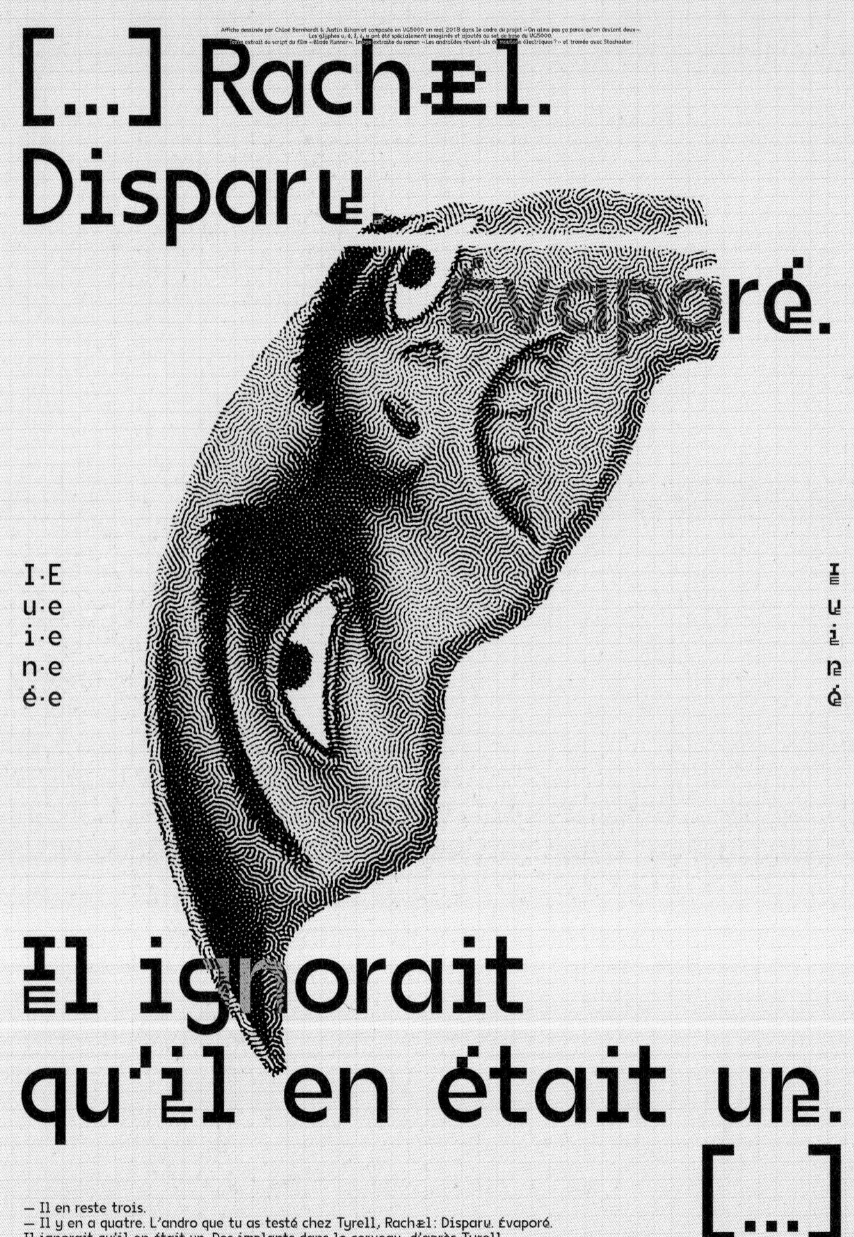
Affiche dessinée par Chloé Bernhardt & Justin Bihan et composée en VG5000 en mai 2018 dans le cadre du projet «On aime pas ça parce qu'on devient deux».
Les glyphes u, é, I, i, n ont été spécialement imaginés et ajoutés au set de base du VG5000.
Texte extrait du script du film «Blade Runner». Image extraite du roman «Les androïdes rêvent-ils de moutons électriques?» et tramée avec Stochaster.
[...] Rachæl.
Disparu.
évaporé.
I·E
u·e
i·e
n·e
é·e
Il ignorait
qu'il en était un.
[...]
— Il en reste trois.
— Il y en a quatre. L'andro que tu as testé chez Tyrell, Rachæl: Disparu. évaporé.
Il ignorait qu'il en était un. Des implants dans le cerveau, d'après Tyrell.

04. VG5000

VG5000 is a set of experimental identification symbols designed to promote the "inclusive rules for writing". It advocates to play down the gender expression difference in French. The designer imagines these glyphs as part of the gendered writing project in graphic ideography initiated by the artist Roxane Maillet.

These new glyphs are developed within the existing frame, featuring the same characteristics but with smaller size.

TD: Justin Bihan
F: Velvetyne Type Foundry

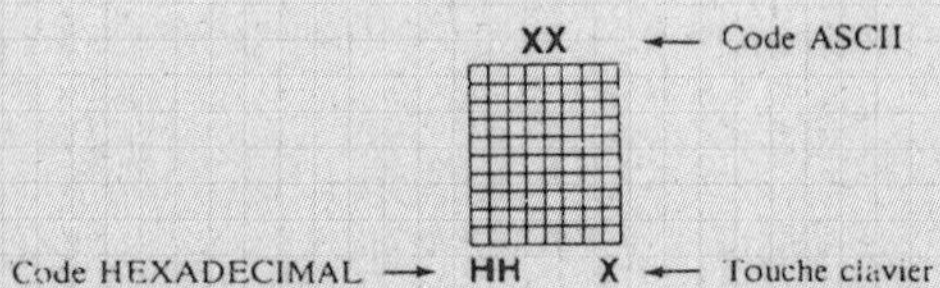

Code ASCII	Code HEXADECIMAL	Touche clavier
0	0	
1	1	
2	2	
3	3	
4	4	
5	5	
6	6	
7	7	
8	8	
9	9	
10	A	
11	B	
12	C	
13	D	
14	E	
15	F	
16	10	••
17	11	-
18	12	é
19	13	ù
20	14	ï
21	15	ç
22	16	û
23	17	à
24	18	â
25	19	è
26	1A	ô
27	1B	ê
28	1C	£
29	1D	
30	1E	
31	1F	
32	20	
33	21	!
34	22	
35	23	#
36	24	$
37	25	%
38	26	&
39	27	;
40	28	(
41	29	)
42	2A	*
43	2B	+
44	2C	,
45	2D	−
46	2E	.
47	2F	÷
48	30	0
49	31	1
50	32	2
51	33	3
52	34	4
53	35	5
54	36	6
55	37	7

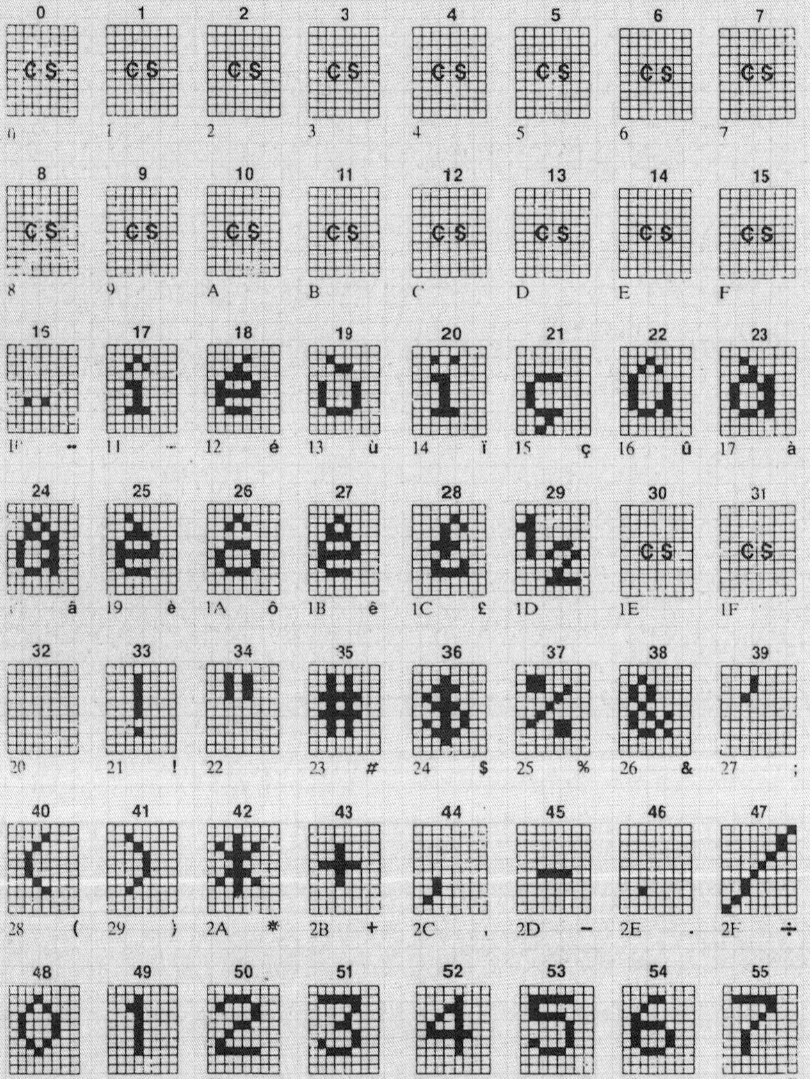

Les

-ils de ?

Qu'est-ce que tu fais ?

, je te .

Comment je suis ?

.

C'est tout ?

Tu es .

Merci.

6 Répliquants : 3 ♂, 3 ♀.

Ils se sont des colonies il y a 2 .

Ils ont 23 et une navette.

Le a été près de la côte.

05. EARTHLAB SANS

Tippet Rise Art Center Rebrand

EarthLab Sans is a customized typeface for the Tippet Rise Art Center. The grid-based typeface is used in posters, brochures and the guide system for exhibitions.

TD&D: Kenneth Kuh
DA: ArtCenter College of Design
CL: Tippet Rise Art Center

INTERACTIVE ARCHITECTURE LAB 2019

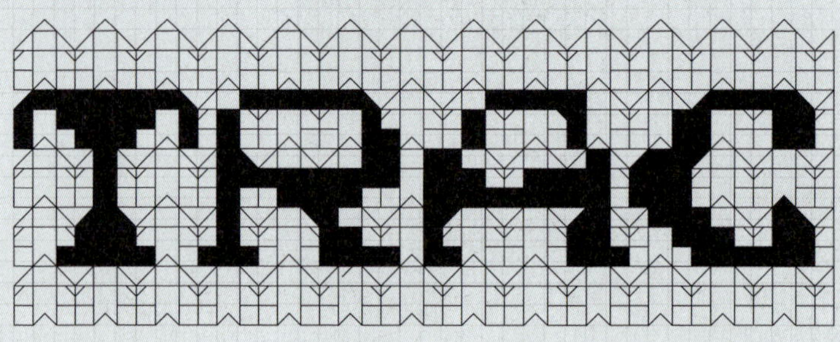

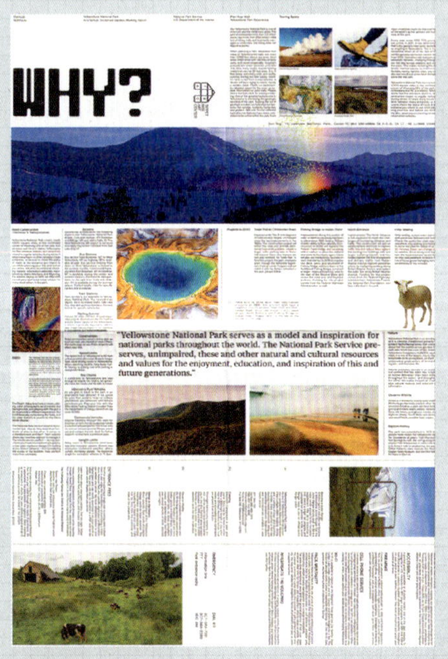
WHY?

"Yellowstone National Park serves as a model and inspiration for national parks throughout the world. The National Park Service preserves, unimpaired, these and other natural and cultural resources and values for the enjoyment, education, and inspiration of this and future generations."

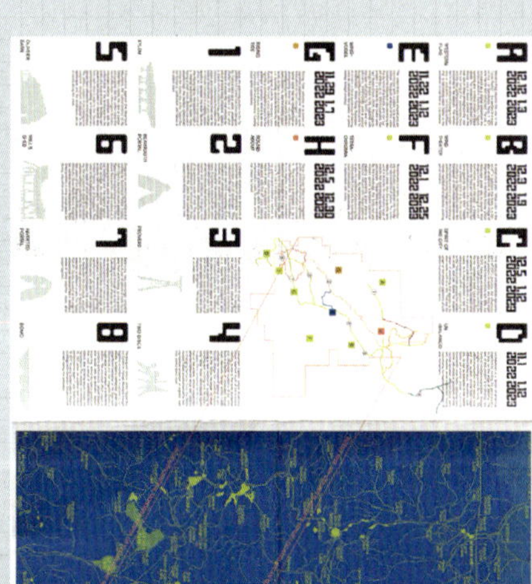

Tippet Rise Art Center, located in the Yellowstone National Park, USA, is surrounded by natural landscapes with rivers and mountains. It is in this unique location that the Art Center blends cultural and natural features to provide visitors with distinctive experience of indoor and outdoor activities. Inspired by this, the designer is dedicated to presenting the integration of cultural geography and art by the design of fonts linkage, introducing its indoor music performances and outdoor hiking adventures, and creating an immersive visual experience.

To make it easy for visitors to distinguish between indoor and outdoor activities, the designer develops two sets of typeface with flexibility and applies them to posters and visually oriented system to create an organic and interesting visual system. Apart from attracting attention rapidly, the visual identification system is required to spread the core values to enhance the depth of brand awareness of the Art Center.

Art measures the human soul," Peter Halstead says. "Novels measure the ability of people to feel. Works of music measure the ability of people to think in ways that aren't verbal. Painting says things that can not be said in prose.

public admissions free
hikigng.Biking free
music events 10 usd
TIPPET
RISE
11.
9.
2022
VISIT WWW.TRAC.ORG
FOR MORE INFO
TICKETS AVAILABLE @
TICKETS.TRAC.ORG
JOHN GERRARD Western Flag December 12 –January 3
FUTURE FARMERS Wind Theater December 3 –January 9
INTERACTIVE ARCH LAB (Un)Balance November 1 –January 12
DAAN ROOSEGAARDE Windvogel November 22 –January 12
1.
22.
2023
UNIVERSAL EVERYTHING Tetrachromia December 1 –December 25
THE CROSS ROADS PROJECT Rising Tide November 29 –January 7
GREEN MEME Green Roundabout December 5 –December 30
CHICO MACMURTRIE Robotic Church January 17 –January 22
ART
CENTER
EARTH
LAB 2022
T R A C

Rule-based Exaggeration

Cycles
Eirene
Galaxy
Mimas
Tarvos
Pandia
Maglev
Sauron
Vostok
Saturn
Gravity
Europa
Rocket
Leucus

06. TROIS MILLE (3000)

The designer Marc Rouault has created the typeface *Trois Mille (3000)* since he worked on his Master Degree's final project at the Royal Academy of Art, The Hague (KABK). Starting from the exploration of research directions, he tried some tools found in the research process, including a broad nib pen commonly used in calligraphy for it facilitates high contrast letterforms (the contrast between thin and thick strokes) . When the nib is set to a fixed angle between 30 and 40 degrees, it can create higher contrast and bolder letterforms. The wider the nib is, the more contrasting the stroke would be drawn.

TD: Marc Rouault
F: Sharp Type Co.

sepulcrat

Factures payer double

absolument pas?

DOIGTURES

amérique Californie

ambient R

arrivent les premiers au garage!

anticiper

ARGUMENTS BITUME

ZENITHQ5112683

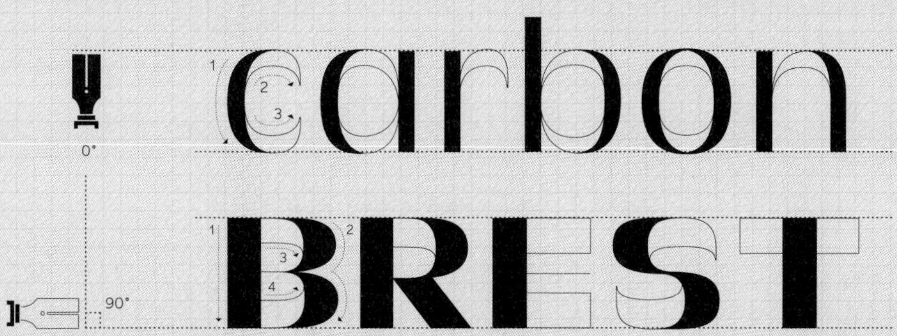

The designer experimented with different tools, for example, to create a low-contrast typeface (with the strokes of same thickness) by setting the brush at the angles between 0 and 90-degree. He found that the only difference lies in the thinner connections of different elements of the strokes. When the strokes are at their thickest, some of the inner parts remain thin, such as the middle bar of "E" and "S". It is the negative space that makes the typeface look more eye-catching.

Meanwhile, all strokes mostly end with vertical lines. The feature is similar to such humanist sans-serif typefaces as *Gill Sans* and *Antique Olive*. *Trois Mille* reinterprets and brings new vitality into the classic typefaces by highlighting more extreme features for weight and width.

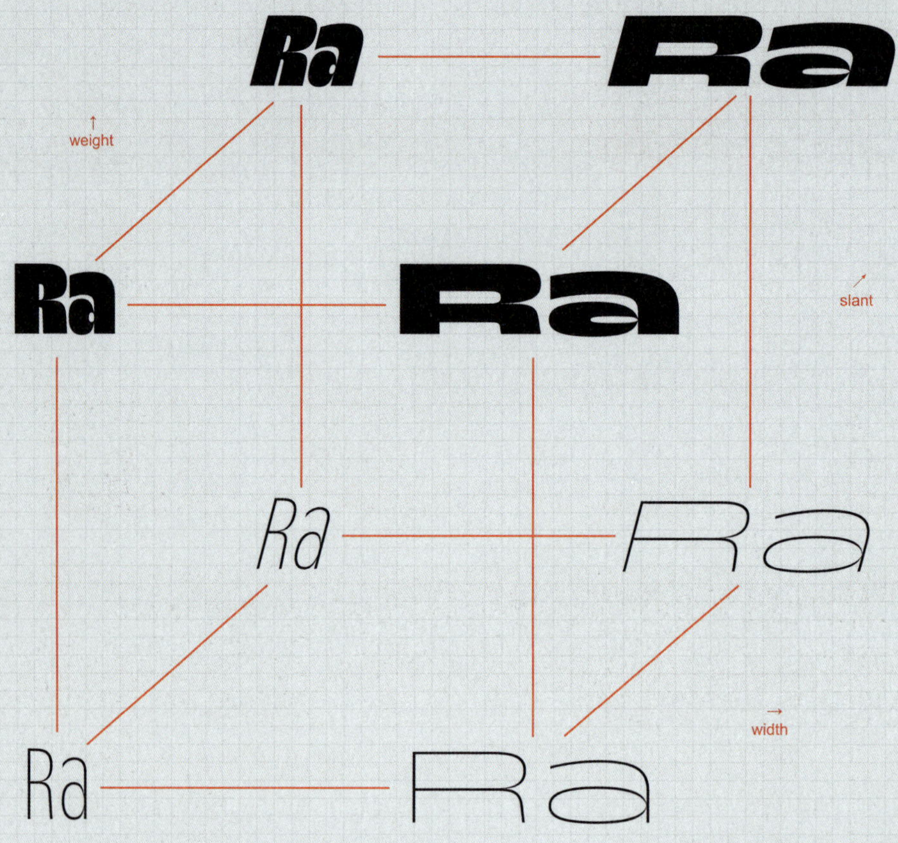

Super-ellipse Axis allows users to tweak the width, weight, slant and other parameters arbitrarily with no limitation.

With no intention of creating a complete font family in the first place, the designer made the Super-ellipse Axis, within which the width, weight and slop could be adjusted arbitrarily, and the ideal style could be selected within the range of the design model. These techniques have been around since the late 1990s, such as the design method of Multiple Master Fonts and TrueTypeGX.

Erik van Blokland, the mentor of the designer, held that such techniques would be back to popular. Under such influence, the designer used the technique in the typeface *Trois Mille*.

A few months after his graduation, the system of Variable Fonts was unveiled at the Association Typographique Internationale held in Warsaw. Although back to the industry, the technology remains at the stage of development. *Trois Mille* has also taken the opportunity to release a font family with numerous instances of variety. As the designer excitedly said, it is a set of fonts developed with Static Variable.

Brochures and Posters of Visual Brand Design for Theatre
DA: Brest Brest Brest
CL: Malraux.

Malraux. Saison 2019 2020

18

Nosferatu

Murnau, Worms, Kummer

19

Malraux. scène nationale Chambéry Savoie 2019 2020
04 79 85 55 43 malrauxchambery.fr
67 place François Mitterrand 73000 Chambéry

DANS LES CORDES (ENTRAILLES)

Pauline Ribat

théâtre création

05 — 08 nov. 20h

Théâtre Dullin Chambéry

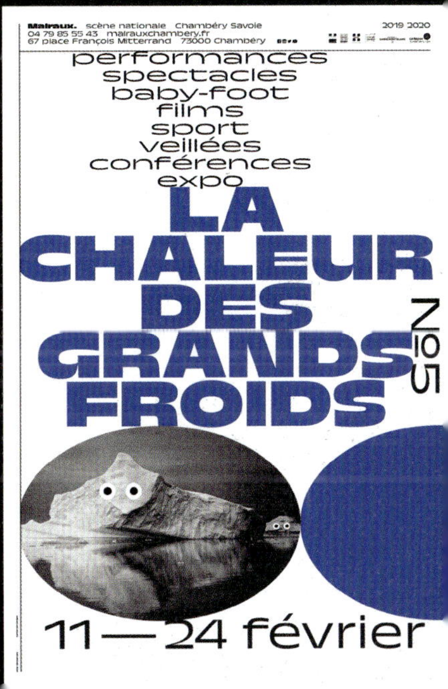

Malraux. scène nationale Chambéry Savoie 2019 2020
04 79 85 55 43 malrauxchambery.fr
67 place François Mitterrand 73000 Chambéry

performances
spectacles
baby-foot
films
sport
veillées
conférences
expo

LA CHALEUR DES GRANDS FROIDS

№5

11 — 24 février

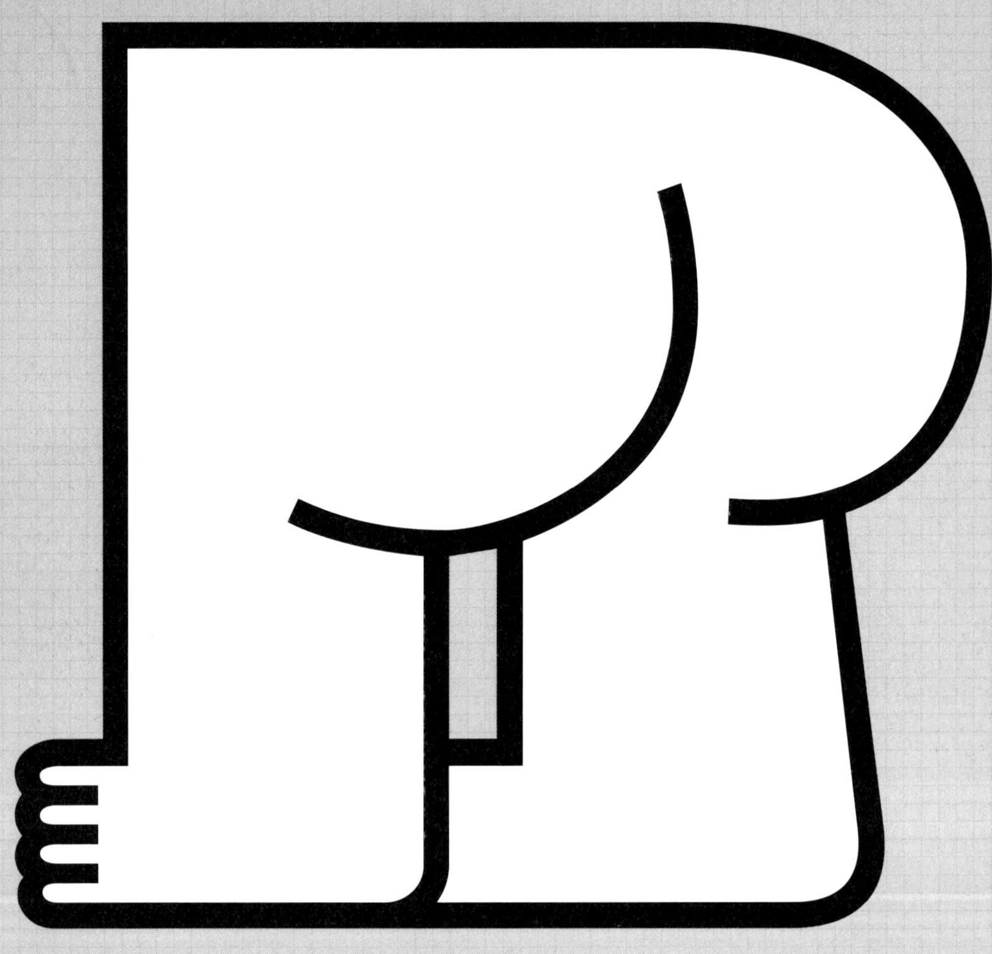

07. TYPEFESSE

Typefesse, which means “type of hip”. The designer is inspired by one or more parts of the human body based on years of drawing sketches. It reflects the beauty and interest of contortions. The body shape is embedded in it as if there is a restless beast tries to jump out of the frame to disturb the readability with surplus energy.

TD: Océane Juvin
F: Velvetyne Type Foundry

PLEURNICHARDS DE CRANACH, LES CULS PARALLÉLÉPIPÉDIQUES DU PICASSO CUBISTE, LES CULS LONGS ET FLEXIBLES DE MODIGLIANI, LES CULS EXOTIQUES ET BIEN ROULÉS DE GAUGUIN, LES CULS MALICIEUX DE FRAGONARD, LES CULS MORBIDES DE LA RÉSURRECTION DE SIGNORELLI, LES CULS RUSTIQUES MAIS PERVERS D'INGRES, LES CULS SOMPTUEUX DE TINTORRET, LES CULS SUGGESTIFS DE POUSSIN, LES CULS GRACIEUSEMENT BALANCÉS DE MAILLOL, LES CULS ENCULÉS DE MOORE, LES CULS ÉPANOUIS DE RENOIR, LES CULS ÉTRIQUÉS DE DUBUFFET, LES CULS NERVEUX DE GOYA, LES CULS ANGULEUX DE HOLBEIN, LES CULS RATATINÉS DE BRUEGEL, LES CULS LYRIQUES DE CHASSÉRIAUX, LES CULS EXHUBÉRANTS DE BELLMER, LES CULS FAROUCHES DE MATISSE, LES CULS VULGAIRES DE TOULOUSE-LAUTREC, LES CULS ÉVIDÉS DE GIACOMETTI, LES CULS INTRÉPIDES DE SCHIELE, LES CULS DÉFIGURÉS DE MAGRITTE, LES CULS INSOLANTS DE SALAVOR DALI, LES CULS ÉNORMES DE LIEPSIGS, LES CULS DIFORMES DE

VALLOTON

The tension of the body symbols is exposed to imply that the readers are playing the role of priers. The designer considers the typeface to intermingle breakthrough and flexibility, with body parts and glyphs defining each other. *Typefesse* creates an air of confusion with the interaction of reading, viewing and peeping and re-establishes the relationship. Designed for headings, it is surprisingly readable when used as a text type.

Typefesse
Pleine

Typefesse est un caractère typographique callipyge dessiné par Océane Juvin et distribué par Velvetyne.

Les stickers sur cette affiche ont été composés par : Nathalie Almange, Ariel Martín Pérez & Anton Moglia.

HISTOIRES DE FESSES
OCÉANE JUVIN & VELVETYNE 2019
TYPEFESSE EST UN CARACTÈRE TYPOGRAPHIQUE CALLITYGE DESSINÉ PAR OCÉANE JUVIN ET DISTRIBUÉ PAR VELVETYNE
CES PAGES RACONTENT SON HISTOIRE, EXPLIQUENT SA CRÉATION ET EXPOSENT SES FORMES CULOTTÉES AUX CÔTÉS D'UN ÉCHANTILLON LITTÉRAIRE ET PICTURAL CHOISI
9 782956 414414
HISTOIRES DE FESSES
Ils arrangent leurs attributs humains de manière plus ou moins contorsionnée.
Au fur-et-à-mesure de la sélection scripturale, ils se réduisent ou s'augmentent.
Calligraphiés, peints, dessinés ou gribouillés. Inspirés par l'art, et jouant avec. Les
ROLAND TOPOR, 1986
dessins de Roland Topor, qui plie le corps humain aux
FESTYPES
émotions qu'il veut susciter, le déforme, le déchire, le coupe, le taille.
Pablo Picasso,
Henri Matisse et leur symbolisme.
Osvaldo Cavandoli,
qui fait vivre un personnage caractériel d'une simple ligne. Les jeux graphiques de Saul Steinberg. Les anges-messagers
HISTOIRES DE FESSES
GLYPHSET
TYPEFESSE OBSCURE
GLYPHSET
TYPEFESSE CLAIRE
TYPEFESSE

Shiloumi
Hanami
Ikigai
Inemuri
Wasaloi
Hijacked

08. TABI SUPER

Consisting of two contrasting fonts, *Tabi Regular* and *Tabi Super*, the typeface *Tabi* is derived from the designer's research topic "Font Family Out of Your Comfort Zone", and the designer gets inspiration from the works of Swedish sculptor Lars Englund. The design of the two fonts epitomizes the concept of binary opposition: thick and bright, highly recognizable and blurry. The typeface focuses on keeping the balance between recognizable functional fonts and obscure graphical forms.

TD: Carolina Festa
F: The Designers Foundry

abc

nae

aTm

Outset Web Design

DA: Kind Studio (London)

Tabi Super looks rough and visually confusing, as if being inflated. The designer uses the functional concept of Ink Trap[①] to make up for the visual effect. *Tabi Regular*, a counterbalance to *Tabi Super*, seems more relevant to the aesthetics of daily life and much lighter, which serves as a foil to *Tabi Super*'s deviation from the path of righteousness.

Before the advent of the high-definition information age, the techniques widely used in newspaper printing and the type design in the digital age created a connection across time and space and media. *Tabi Super* provides a good example of looking to the past for inspiration.

Usually, Ink Trap is only used for small-sized printed text. Its application in *Tabi Super* is not for the purpose of functionality, but to meet the requirements of type modeling and decoration.

① Ink Trap is a type processing technique in which the edges of the printed text are blurred by the removal of corners of the fonts to prevent ink from soaking into each other.

Rule-based Exaggeration

09. NRV

Hip Dozer Compilation Vol. IV

Hip Dozer is a French record label that is dedicated to breaking away from stereotype and creating a new hip-hop collection cover to embrace a visual makeover.

The main visual *NRV* typeface for the album cover was created in a type design workshop. The designer experimented with using only scissor and papers to make words. It was originally to create a font with serif bold and big enough to write inside. Meanwhile, the designer's preference for the old wooden type and the urban dialect type has brought inspiration to the font designing process which is much the same way that music is produced. It requires recording, clipping and editing as well. The difference is that musicians play with invisible sounds.

TD: Hugo Mut
CL: Hip Dozer Label

no

tocard

i a

no
NRV.otf
Stroke endings: Serifs,
Weight: Bold ,
Width: Extended,
Contrast: A lot,
Construction: Roma
tocard
i a

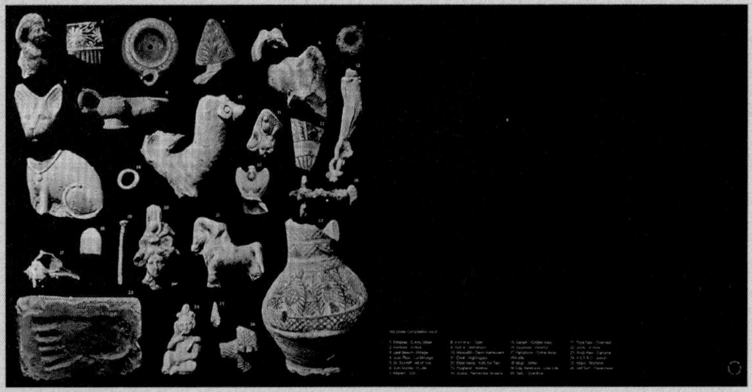

Like metronomic designer, when designing frames and ornaments, the designer found a large number of forgotten patterns in the font samples from the Deberny-Peignot catalogue and applied them as decorations in the design. The vinyl inside pages are partly inspired by archaeological books, with each antique representing the artists and their musical works.

There is no lack of archeological elements to the overall design, and through it is the declaration that hip-hop, an art form that requires constant Digging and Sampling, has become a living fossil of modern culture.

Part 2.
BITMAP

Design Language

10. NORD MONO

The designer is very much in love with minimalism, and draws a lot of creative inspiration from 20th-century minimalist designers such as Wim Crouwel and Mimmo Castellano. *Nord Mono* is one of the many designers who have experimented with fonts. As the fonts convey information, readability is key for most projects, and fonts are a vehicle for emotional communication and expression.

TD: Shamil Asgarov

ABCDE
FGHIJ
KLMNO
PQRST
UVWXY
Z..

The designer who made the name as an illustrator determined the horizontal elements and the combination of fonts in the creation for the first place, and then built a grid system of layout and made adjustments according to the specific project. There are many benefits to follow the preset rules.

The designer used this font to convey emotion, give voice to information, and set a unique form and style for it.

11. TURNOVER

Turnover is not only a typeface, but also a series of graphics and symbols. The set of aequilatus fonts is based on a basic square grid. The overall style features are reflected in the strong contrast between the glyphs and the black-white layering. The simple grid features make it easy to create a variety of bold layouts.

DA: My Name is Wendy
TD&D: Carole Gautier, Eugénie Favre

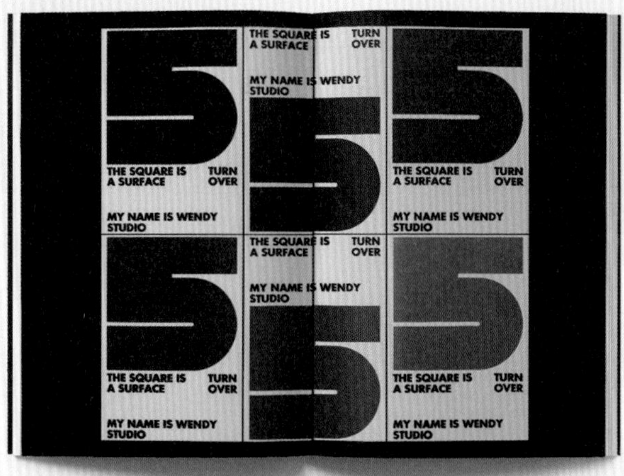
THE SQUARE IS A SURFACE
TURN OVER
MY NAME IS WENDY STUDIO

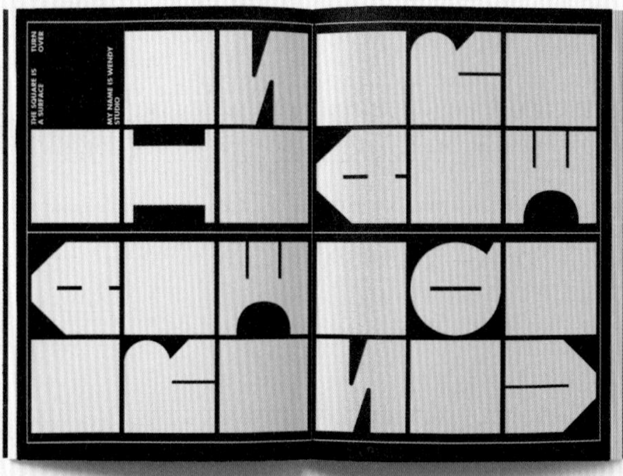
THE SQUARE IS A SURFACE
TURN OVER
MY NAME IS WENDY STUDIO

TURN OVER
THE SQUARE IS A SURFACE
MY NAME IS WENDY STUDIO
THE SQUARE IS A SURFACE
TURN OVER
MY NAME IS WENDY STUDIO

THE SQUARE IS
A SURFACE
MY NAME IS WENDY
STUDIO
THE SQUARE IS
A SURFACE
MY NAME IS WENDY
STUDIO
TURNOVER
TYPEFACE
TYPOGRAPHY
LETTERING
LAYOUT
MY NAME IS WENDY
GRAPHIC DESIGN
ART DIRECTION

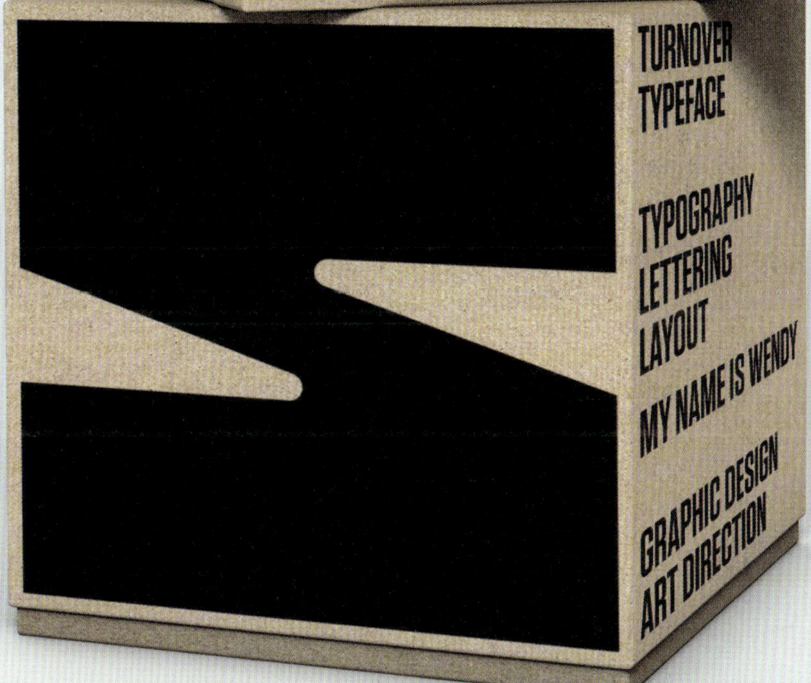
TURNOVER
TYPEFACE
TYPOGRAPHY
LETTERING
LAYOUT
MY NAME IS WENDY
GRAPHIC DESIGN
ART DIRECTION

12. KOBATA

Although the pixel fonts are emerging in large numbers, the designer intends to buck the trend by creating the fonts that differ from the present aesthetic, such as the circles or rectangles of different proportions within a font family. The typeface *Kobata* is born at the right moment, considered more likely to be an art of type than a design element. To avoid overriding the theme, the designer evenly distributes the circular elements in *Kobata*, creating the impression of raindrops falling on a paddy field. The typeface is ideal to be used in digital art.

TD: Ariel Martín Pérez

The Chevigny City Hall Orchestra presents:

A concert by the Polyphonic Choir of Maspalomas

ORPHEUS AND EURYDICE

Mercredi 16 juillet - à partir de 18h

136 rue de Raimans

www.chevigny.com

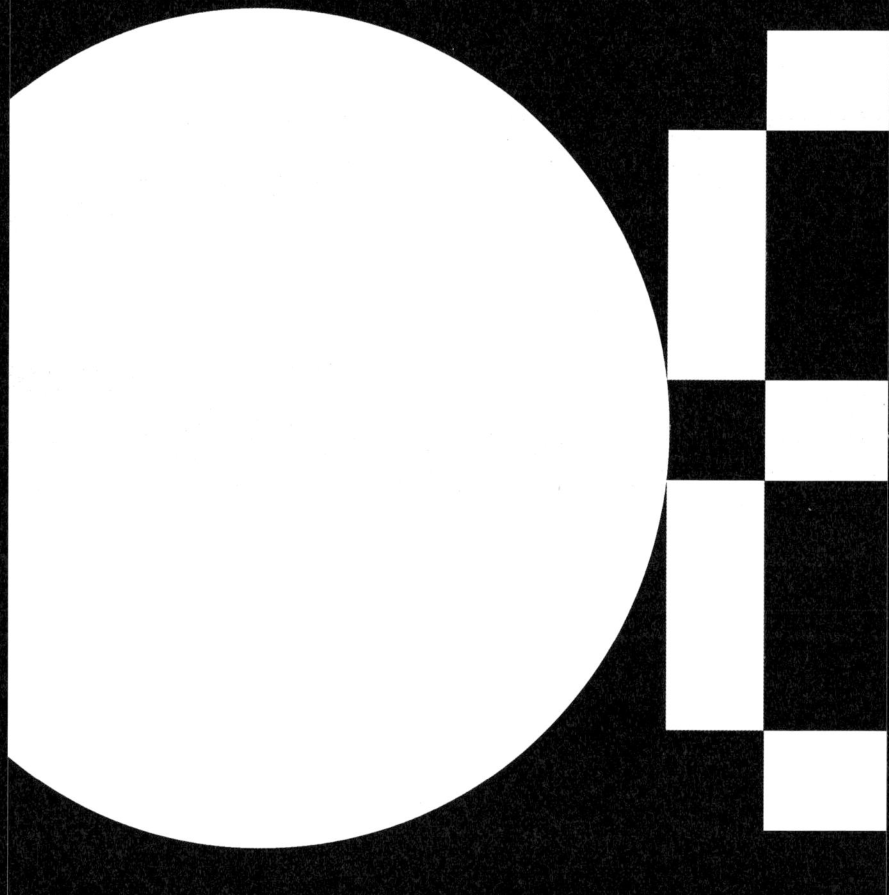

72 pts

Data.Syntax (Vit Dataplex)

48 pts

Ryoji Ikeda, 2007

24 pts

Quick fox jumps nightly above wizard. A very bad quack might jinx zippy fowls.

The typeface was inspired by the “Ichimatsu Moyo”, a chequered pattern popular in Japan during the Edo period. It consists of two regular shapes connected at right angles or lines that are not optically corrected, except for circles. Coincidentally, *Kobata* bears a striking resemblance to some Japanese logos from the 1980s.

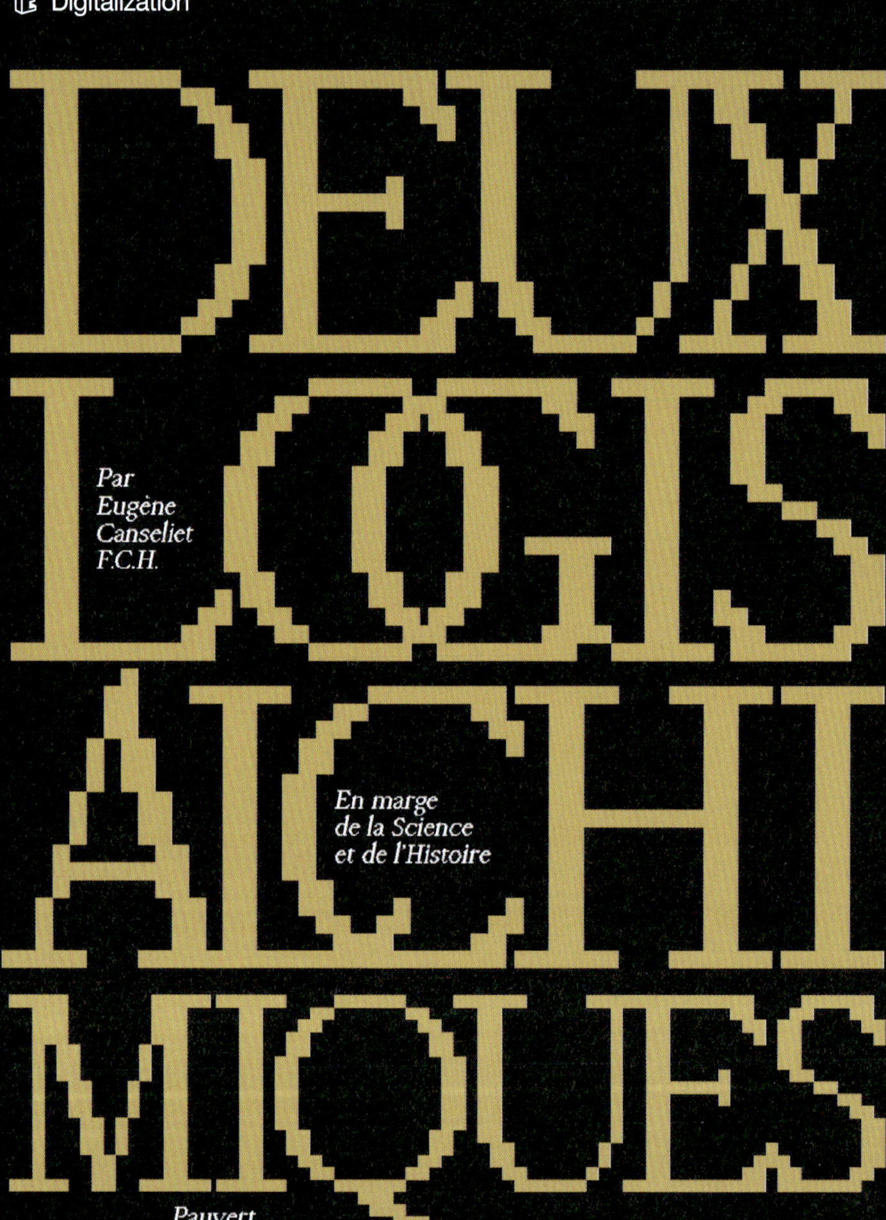
Digitalization
DEUX LOGIS ALCHIMIQUES
Par
Eugène
Canseliet
F.C.H.
En marge
de la Science
et de l'Histoire
Pauvert

13. MONDWEST & NEUEBIT TYPEFACES

This set of pixel fonts has great potential for development, inspired by the classic sans serifs and serifs in recent times. It comprises more than 600 characters, symbols, and icons of four styles, possessing a high degree of readability, versatility, and fitness after elaborate design.

Digital processing aims to re-imagine more possibilities for the type styles, pushing these timeess classics of the typefaces towards a more representational futuristic or brutalist style.

TD: Steve Marchal x Pangram Pangram® Foundry (PP®F)
F: Pangram Pangram® Foundry

AaBbCc

Mondwest™ Reg レグラレ
Bitmap Display Typeface
⚠Monday 04.20.2020
at PangramPangram®
<Datalaze™><PP®F>
☽←CA✧EU→☼

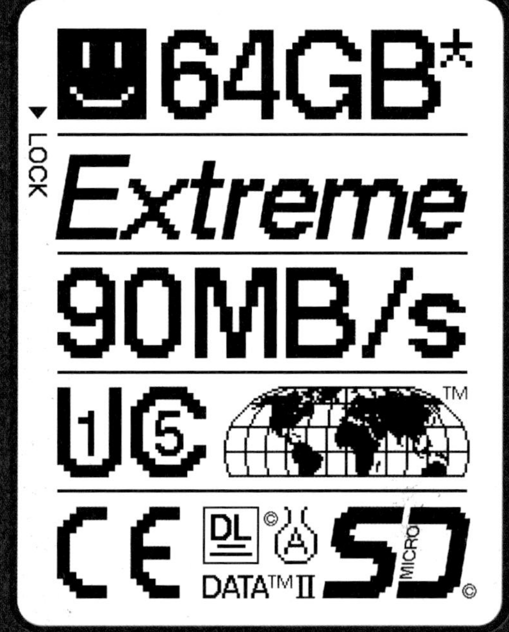

NeueBit™
BoldCE
280pt600
Gl. .OTF-

¶AaBbCc
→12345
Pangram²
CA — CE

NeueBit™
BoldCE
280pt600
Gl. .OTF-

¶AaBbCc
→12345
Pangram²
CA — CE

14. PLAY

Landscape for the Game

Play is a modular typeface designed as a space of Landscape for the Game for the children[1]. The Playground makes the urban form reduced into the interior, where the structure and geometry match the colorful floor patterns, to facilitate the imaginations of the children and adults to play freely.

Starting with pixel letters, the designer attempts to incorporate the geometry of the game space into the typeface, while keeping it simple and readable. In addition to the basics style, the designer creates another demo version, where a part of the grid pixels is pulled out and replaced with another geometric shape to add more colors. This method has enlarged the space while increasing the fonts from the demo version, suitable for the design of souvenirs. The basic style can be applied to all information texts and smaller carriers.

TD&D: Dasha Levchuk

① Landscape for the Game is located in the cultural center of Mattadero, Spain, and designed by Aberrant Architecture.

LANDSCAPE FOR THE GAME

A playground of Aberrant Architecture

COM
ING
SOON

Part 3.
BE CONNECTED

Design Language

15. THE VIOLENCE OF LANGUAGE

As for the typeface for accusing of language violence, the designer starts from the interaction between adults and children, with regular scripts as the basic glyphs, and dots as the symbol of the head. The abusive language is like an invisible knife to a childish heart, causing irreparable wounds. The designer hopes to remind people through this figurative artistic processing that the insult of spoken language to the heart is irreversible and irreparable.

TD&D: Xu Hanming

LANGUAGE
VIOLENCE
语言暴力
MON
31.10.18
NO 1
PIG BRAIN
OF
CHILD
PRESSURE
孩子压力

LANGUAGE
VIOLENCE
语言暴力

MON
31.10.18

NO 4

逼死人 TORTURED

CMYK 300dpi

OF
CHILD
PRESSURE
孩子压力

16. DINKIE BITMAP

Dinkie Bitmap is a pixel-style typeface. It challenges the smallest bitmap Chinese font. The font also supports Latin, Greek, Cyrillic letters, Japanese, Arabic and Hebrew. The Java and Mongolian are under development as well.

TD: Willie Liu
F: 3type

16 pixel grid Chinese Typeface

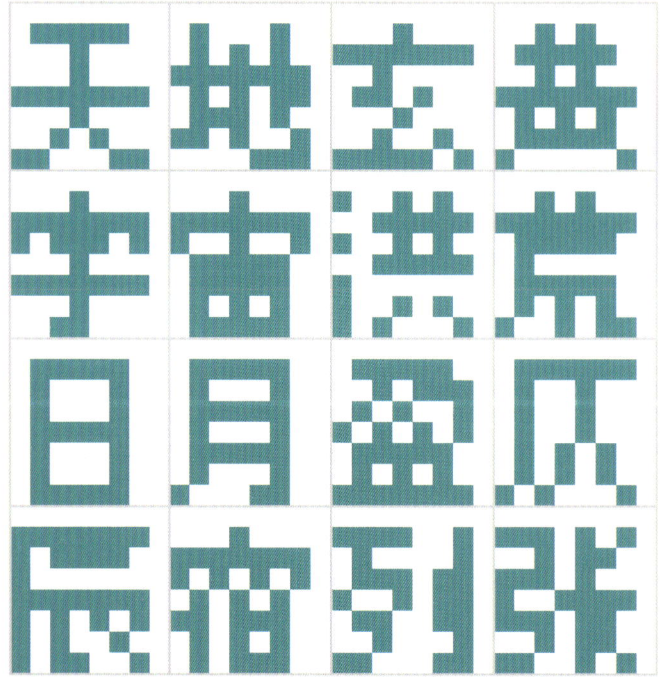

DINKIE BITMAP

橘子 ← 橘子

7PX

我说道：「爸爸，你走吧。」他望车外看了看，说：「我买几个橘子去。你就在此地，不要走动。」我看那边月台的栅栏外有几个卖东西的等着顾客。走到那边月台，须穿过铁道，须跳下去又爬上去。父亲是一个胖子，走过去自然要费事些。我本来要去的，他不肯，只好让他去。

铁道 ← 铁道

9PX

我说道：「爸爸，你走吧。」他望车外看了看，说：「我买几个橘子去。你就在此地，不要走动。」我看那边月台的栅栏外有几个卖东西的等着顾客。走到那边月台，须穿过铁道，须跳下去又爬上去。父亲是一个胖子，走过去自然要费事些。我本来要去的，他不肯，只好让他去。

The original purpose of designing *Dinkie Bitmap* is to explore the possibility of small-size pixelated Chinese characters, paying tribute to the pioneers bringing the Chinese language into the information age. However, the complexity of the Chinese characters, compared to the Latin, makes it difficult to display in this way. The designer has found that it is unnecessary to clearly distinguish each stroke in reading Chinese characters, so he reduces and recombines the strokes in designing the typeface, to achieve the small-size pixelation[①].

① *Dinkie Bitmap* contains two sizes of pixel characters, 7 pixel and 9 pixel grid, and challenges the smallest bitmap Chinese typeface.

Dinkie Bitmap

دينكى بتمپ

丁卯点阵体

ディンキービットマップ

→らヂ✦♫☕

丁卯点阵体是一款像素风格的多语言字体

deftly available in 7px and 9px

このフォントは OpenType フォントとして

ゆたかな機能をサポートしています

إنه تعبير عن روح الحنين على الإنترنت

في ظروفنا الخاصة اليوم

החלק הסיני הוא כיסוי על הקריאות של

אותיות סיניות אולטרה-זעירות

(๑•̀ㅂ•́)و✧ (;3[▓▓]

¯_(ツ)_/¯ ≥(￣▭￣≤)

(╯#-_-)╯┴—┴

｡*:☆(・ω・人・ω・)｡:゜☆｡

♪───O(≧∇≦)O────♪

*. ﾟ ﾟ. *:..｡o..｡o:*. ヽ(*ﾟ▽ﾟ*)ﾉ. *:..｡o..｡o:*. ﾟ ﾟ. *

♈ ♉ ♊ ♋ ♌ ♍ ♎ ♏ ♐ ♑ ♒ ♓ ✝ ⛫ ☆ ✂ ☎ ☏ ☺ ☻ ☠

☐ ☑ ☒ ฿ 𝄢 ♩ ♪ ♫ ♬ ♭ ♮ ♯ ✧ ♥ ➛ ↑ ↗ → ↘ ↓ ↙ ← ↖ ⇔ ⇕ ⟲ ⟳

▓ ▓ ▓ ◷ ▢ △ ⚀ ⚁ ⚂ ⚃ ⚄ ⚅ ☉ ☺ ∞ ∫ Π Σ √ ∂

Dinkie Bitmap gives expression to a total of 6,000 characters and symbols. The number keeps growing.

In addition, *Dinkie Bitmap* contains a large number of Unicode symbols and graphics to create vivid and interesting images. It has also made some symbols in particular for emojis, including the Kannada letter "ಥ", the Cyrillic supplementary letter "ꙍ", and the Canadian aboriginal character "ᕙ", sufficient to cover most of the emojis in common use.

This typeface is quite suitable for pixel-style illustrations, animation, games, and such, and also for the non-pixel graphic design and video images, to convey a sense of ease or of sci-tech innovation. The minimum-size pixel can also greatly improve the efficiency of LED displays. Moreover, the fonts made up entirely of straight lines are extremely small to be used as WebFont for the webpages.

17. FLEA MARKET POSTERS

The Sunny Buddy Market and the Full Autumn Market are two flea markets organized by the Korean brand store TWL in spring and autumn respectively. The name of the Markets was first designed with Chinese characters for emphasis. Such type design also signifies the seasons when the Markets are held.

TD: Jaemin Lee
DA: Studio fnt
CL: TWL

이천십오년
춘우장 —
좋은 친구들의
봄날 장터
春
友
場
서울특별시
종로구 연건동
302-8
(율곡로 187)
토토빌딩 주차장
오월 구일
낮
열두시부터
저녁
여섯시까지
그러려니
꿀
당케
더리넨테이블
덴스
명조장
보타라보
비씨커피
서울 르프티
서커스보이밴드
에프앤티
에토프
오와이이
오이뮤
올프로바이더스
워크스
주스토닉
지승민의 공기
코우너스
툴 프레스
티더블유엘
하우아유투데이
호호당
홈그라운드
훈고링고 브레드
春友場

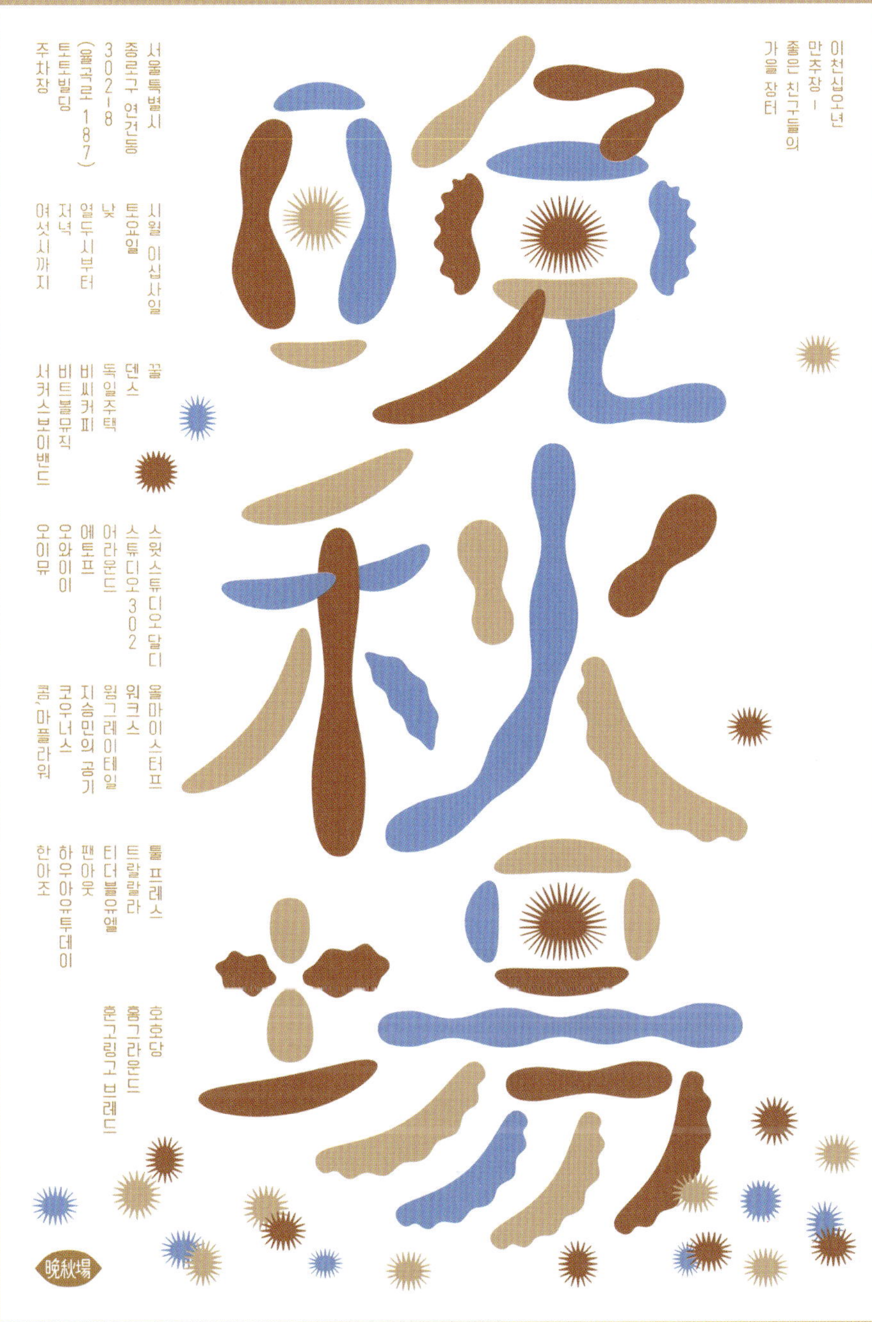
이천십오년
만추장 —
좋은 친구들의
가을 장터
晩秋場
서울특별시
종로구 연건동
302-8
(율곡로 187)
토토빌딩
주차장
시월 이십사일
토요일
낮
열두시부터
저녁
여섯시까지
꿀
덴스
독일주택
비씨커피
비트볼뮤직
서커스보이밴드
스윗스튜디오달디
스튜디오302
어라운드
에토프
오와이이
오이뮤
올마이스터프
웍크스
웜그레이테일
지승민의 공기
코우너스
콤,마플라워
툴 프레스
트랄랄라
티더블유엘
팬아웃
하우아유투데이
한아조
호호당
홈그라운드
훈고링고 브레드
晩秋場

18. CHINESE CALLIGRAPHY IN MODERN STYLE

The designer believes that the typeface is a kind of exploration and attempt. Many people would recombine the strokes selected from the ancient calligraphy to create and develop the characters in another style of writing. In this project, the designer uses the Chinese cursive script to create Chinese characters in a more modern style and takes higher degree of recognition as primary consideration. Each character is written in a single stroke, neat and concise. The proper distribution of joined-up circular and square writing also contributes to the freestyle and fluency and brings the unique sense of dynamic and rhythm that the designer thinks is exclusive to modern fonts.

TD: Xu Hanming

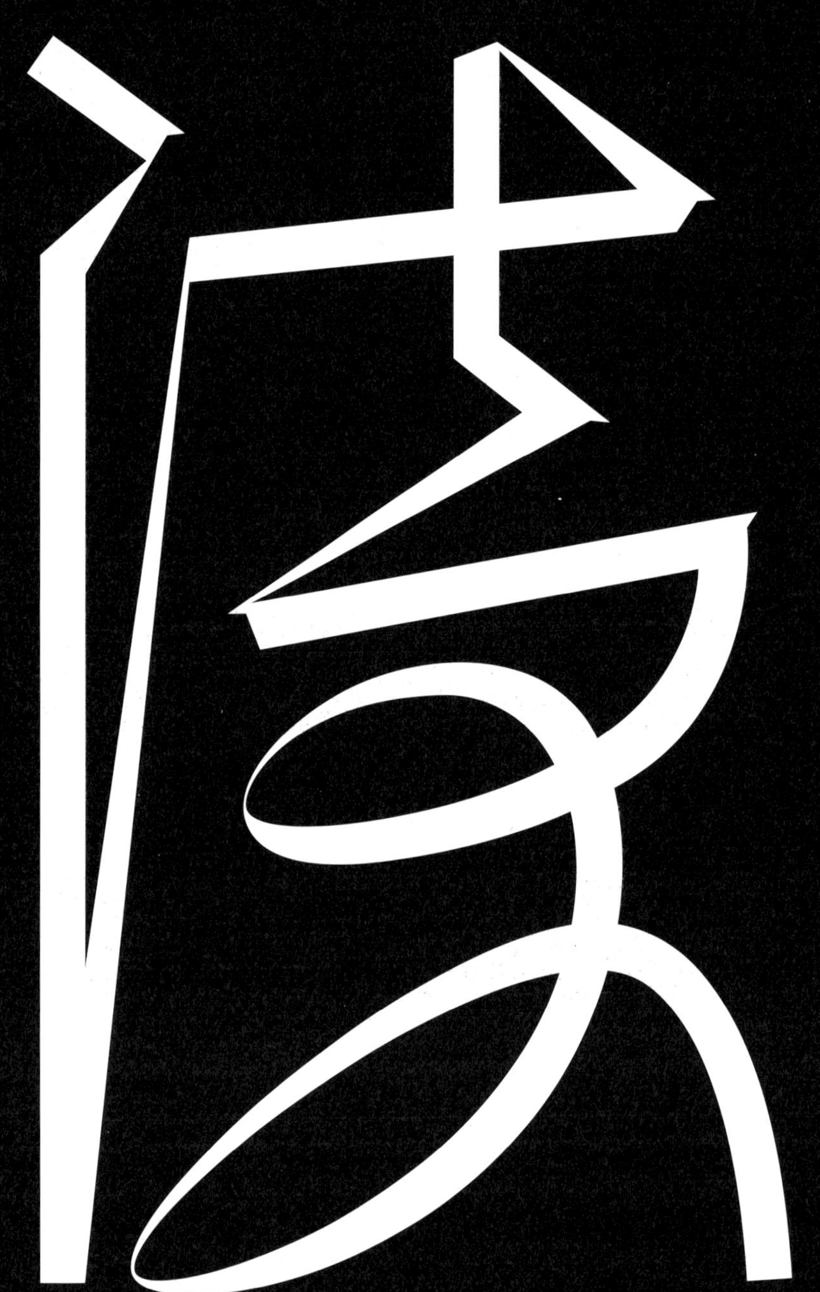

和浅
寂这
地来
和浅
地来

浅浅的笑温和的光线静地
这个空灵清寂的季节坐下
来静读天读地读光阴散落
浅浅的笑温和的光线静地
每一寸毛孔因此都通光线
来静读天读地读光阴散落
浅浅的笑温和的光线静地
这个空灵清寂的季节坐下
来静读天读地读光阴散落
浅浅的笑温和的光线静地
每一寸毛孔因此都通光线
来静读天读地读光阴散落

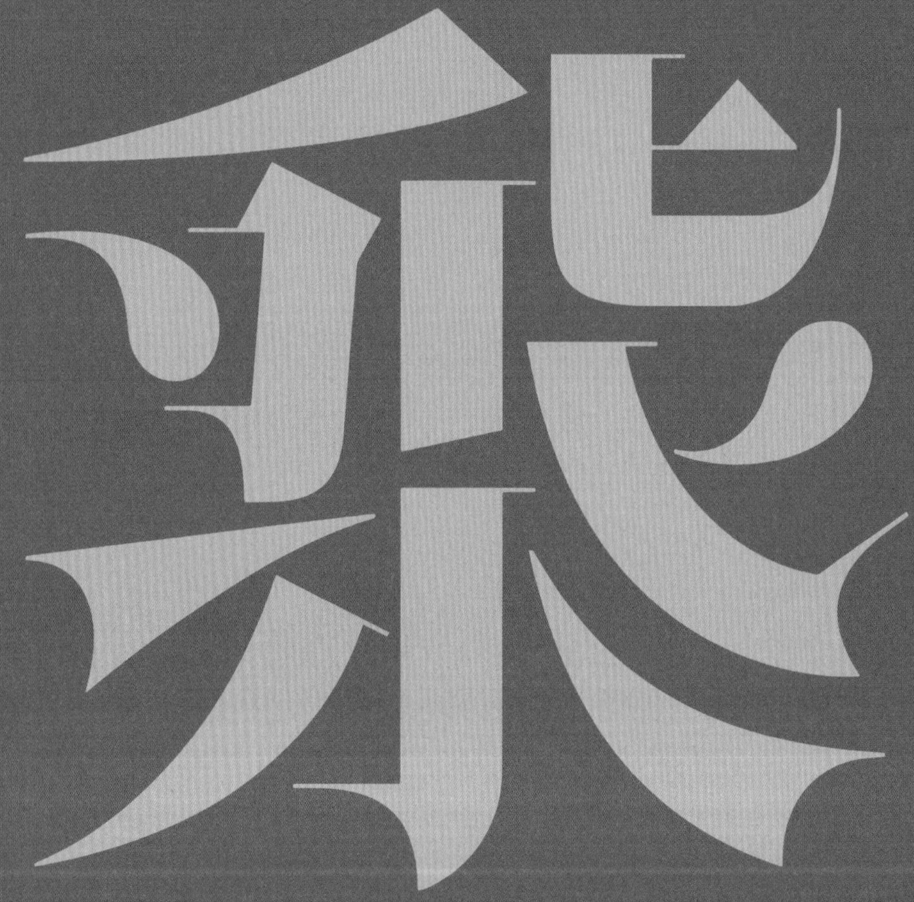
飛

19. MING ROMANTIC™

Ming Romantic™① is a Chinese typeface inspired by typography in the Song and Ming dynasties②. With the innovation of printing technology in this period, the strokes tend to be straighter, featuring strong contrast of thickness. The stylized small triangle at the end of the strokes is regarded as one characteristic.

The overall, more rectilinear form is known as craftsman script and is the basis of all descendent Songti style forms. Following this historical heritage, *Ming Romantic*™ explores the possibilities of font development. The final work makes a sharp contrast based on strengthening the characteristics of Song typeface, which is suitable for display as well.

TD: Synoptic Office
DA: Synoptic Office
CL: Retail

① *Ming Romantic*™ made its first debut in a special poster designed by Chris Wu, a partner of the Wkshps, for the exhibition "Point, Line, and Shape". At the invitation of Natasha Jen, a partner of Pentagram, this typeface was officially unveiled at the 7th Ningbo International Design Biennale. It was specially adapted for the Pentagram Remix exhibition in the Biennale, paying tribute to the 40th Anniversary of the founding of Pentagram.

我們的明

我們的明日

我們的明日

White
Dew
白露
Said In A Chinese Lunar Calendar 24 Specific Depth Of Change Of Season,
Is Based On The Position In The Zodiac,
Each Respectively Corresponding To The Earth Every Movement
On The Ecliptic 15° Reach A Certain Position.
CHINA'S
24 SOLAR TERMS
Copyright © Fxckdown All Rights Reserved

20. THE 24 SOLAR TERMS

As a key part of the long history and culture of the Chinese nation, the 24 solar terms embody the historical and cultural essence of the Chinese civilization. The designer created the poster series by looking for the relationship between the Chinese character fonts and the changes in the solar term, climate, and phenological stage, aiming to promote the culture of the 24 solar terms while exploring the type design of Chinese characters.

D: Zhou Shaolong
DA: Fun Vision Studio

GRAIN
IN
EAR
BUSY
PLANTING
CHINA'S
24 SOLAR TERMS
Said In A Chinese Lunar Calendar 24 Specific Depth Of Change Of Season.
Is Based On The Position In The Zodiac.
Each Respectively Corresponding To The Earth Every Movement On The Ecliptic 15° Reach A Certain Position.
Grain In Ear
06.06

CHINA'S 24 SOLAR TERMS
Said in a Chinese lunar calendar 24 specific d... of chang... of season, is based on the position in the z...diac, each re-spectively corresponding to the earth ev... movement on the ecliptic 15 ° reach a certain position
AWAKENING
LOOK FOR FOOD
INSECTS
2019
·
03
06
CHINA'S
24 SOLAR TERMS
Awakening
of Insects
OUT THE HOLE

THE
NATIONAL
ART CENTER,
TOKYO

21. NACT

Visual Identity of The National Art Center, Tokyo

The designer uses the Chinese character " 新 " to represent the general visual image of the National Art Center, Tokyo[①]. Influenced by the Japanese architect Kisho Kurokawa, Kashiwa Sato incorporates the blank space into the visual identity fonts, as well as the English and digital fonts specially designed for the art museum in the sample style. These fonts are used in the visual system and products of art museum. The design series integrate the core values and unique architectural styles of the art museum in the visual system, fully displaying the spirit of liberty and openness represented by the museum.

CL: NACT
DA: Samurai
CD&AD: Kashiwa Sato

① The National Art Center, Tokyo (NACT), founded in 2007, is located in Roppongi. As the fifth largest national art museum in Japan, NACT is unique in that it has no permanent collection and is dedicated to art-related events as exhibition venues, art library, and art education institutions combined.

国立新美術館

THE NATIONAL ART CENTER, TOKYO

国立新美術館

THE NATIONAL
ART CENTER, TOKYO 国立新美術館

ABCDEFGHIJKLMNOPQRS
TUVWXYZ0123456789#
* _ : ; < > [ ] = ! ? - . , + / $ % & ' " @

THE NATIONAL ART CENTER, TOKYO
MUSEUM SHOP + GALLERY
SOUVENIR FROM TOKYO - FROM UNDERGROUND TO MAINSTREAM.
TOKYO IS A RADICAL JUMBLE OF CONTRASTING ELEMENTS WHERE THE NEW
AND NOSTALGIC, THE MOST ELEGANT LUXURY AND EVERYDAY KITSCH,
THE DOMESTIC AND EXOTIC,
THE FAMOUS AND ANONYMOUS ALL EXIST SIDE BY SIDE.

THE CUTTING EDGE MIX WE PRESENT IS A PRODUCT OF OUR ABILITY
TO SEE BEYOND EXISTING ATTITUDES AND CREATE A NEW EDITORIAL PROCESS
THAT REFLECTS THE IMAGINATION,
ENERGY AND CHAOTIC BEAUTY THAT MAKE UP TODAY'S TOKYO
AND ITS ATTITUDE TO ART AND DESIGN.
IN THE SAME WAY JAPAN HAS GIVEN SUSHI AND SUMO TO THE WORLD,
WE NOW PRESENT AN INTERNATIONALLY FLAVORED, BUT TOKYO EDITED,
SOUVENIR FROM TOKYO WWW.CIBONE.COM/SFT

新
THE
TOKYO

无处
不兒童

22. CHILDREN EVERYWHERE

Charity Typography Design

The User Experience Design Department of Tencent, together with the One Foundation, selected the works of 70 artists in the co-creation design “Let Love Replace Grudge”, and arranged the painting exhibition “Children Everywhere”. The exhibition has 27 shops invited to extend the exhibition space to the “window display” outside, to break the spatial boundaries with the help of works and anticipate a more open social environment for the autistic.

D: Peng Cheng

I LOVE
STARS
关爱美丽的心灵
Care for a
beautiful mind
壹基金
One Foundation
腾讯看点
Starry Color
2020.07.17Fri - 07.27Sun
无处
不见童

I LOVE
RAIN
关爱美丽的心灵
Care for a
beautiful mind
无处
不兒童
2020.07.17Fri - 07.26Sun
壹基金
One Foundation
腾讯看点
Starry Color

壹基金
One Foundation
腾讯看点
Starry Color *
I LOVE FRUIT
关爱美丽的心灵
Care for a beautiful mind
2020.07.17Fri - 07.26Sun
无处
不児童

I LOVE
ANIMALS
关爱美丽的心灵
Care for a
beautiful mind
2020.07.17Fri - 07.26Sun
壹基金
One Foundation
腾讯看点
Starry Color *

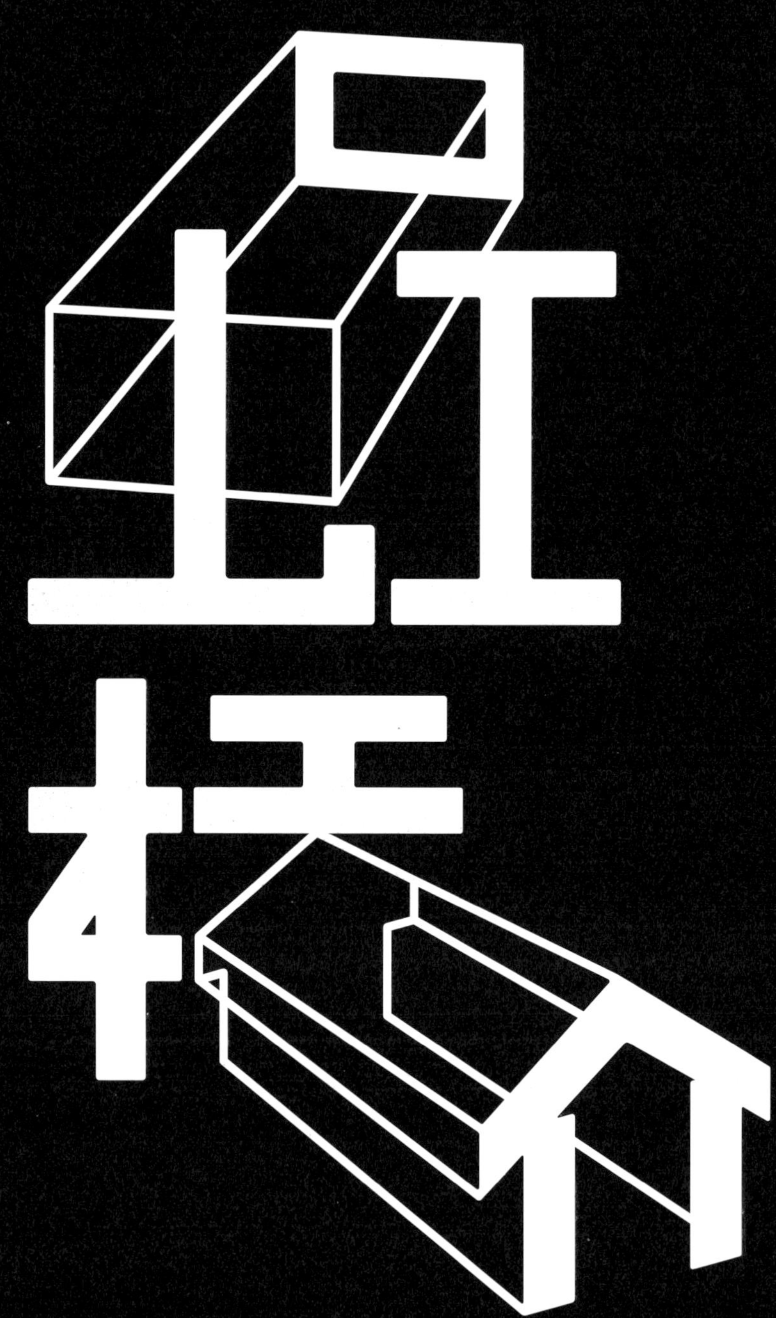

23. CUBIC TYPOGRAPHY

It is a typeface designed for the brand image of the interior studio in Hongqiao, Shanghai. The designer holds that the interior design is a kind of spatial beautification, during which the spatial layout is in constant change, alternating with one another. It is as interesting as a Rubik's Cube. The designer takes it as inspirations to create three-dimensional and structurally diverse spaces for the typeface.

TD: Xu Hanming

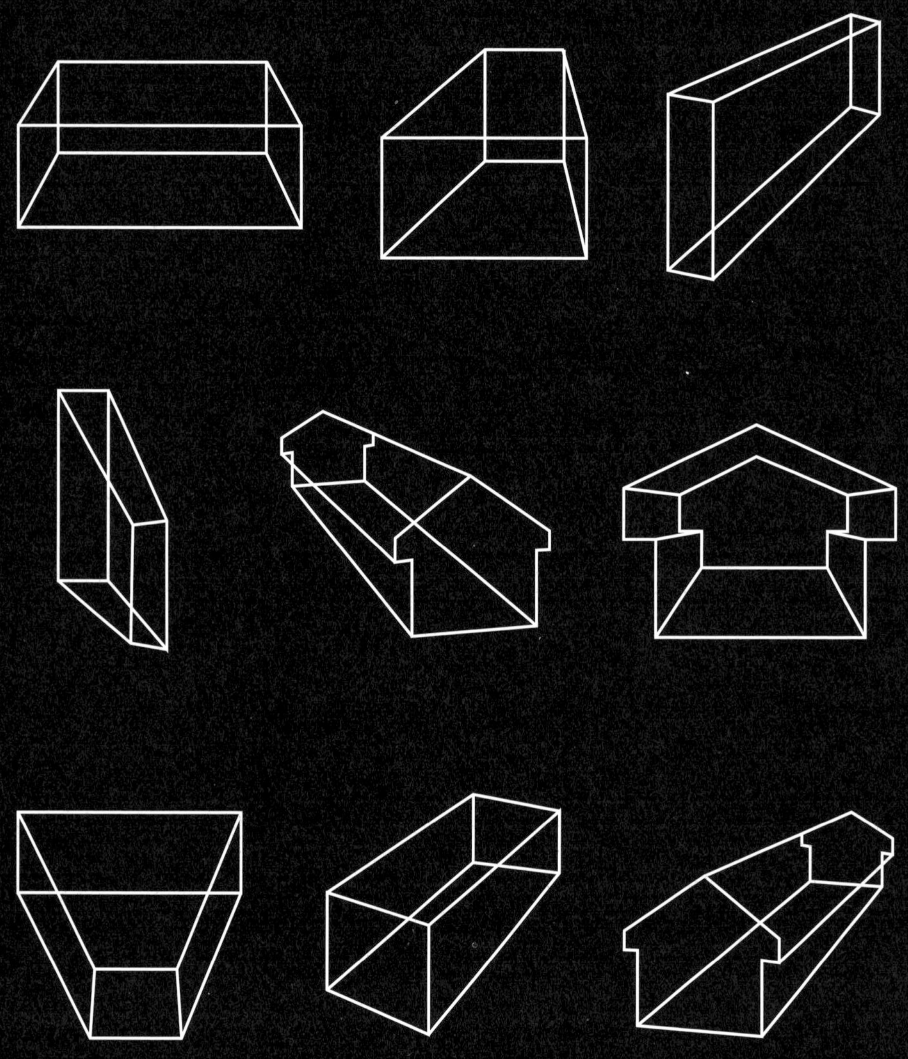

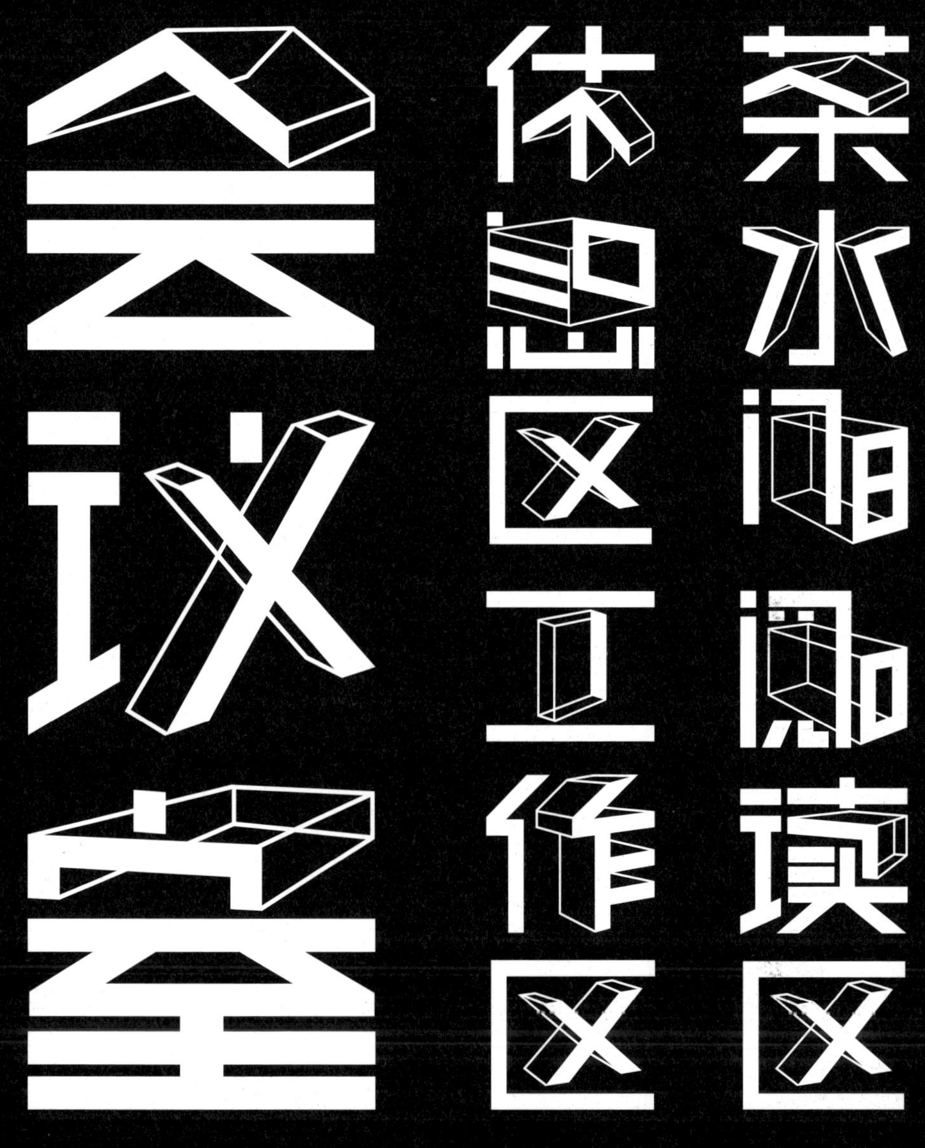
茶水间
阅读区
休息区
工作区
会议室

字的變奏

24. RVS BASIC

RVS Basic is a reverse-contrast font family, designed in the design course on Latin Typefaces held by 3type in late 2019. It boasts of a simple structure, with strong contrast in thickness of the strokes and the iconic dot design.

The reverse-contrast style makes it easy for *RVS Basic* to evolve into a font family with 10 values of width. Without changing the type size, the designer can create a strong visual variation by selecting the fonts of various widths. *RVS Basic* also has rounded fonts. Featured with the sense of retro, fashion, relaxation, tension, comedy, cuteness, toxicity, and such, the typeface has a wide range of uses suitable for both young and old.

TD: Li Zhiqian
F: 3type

基本美术体
RVS Basic

Say 'Reverse' in other languages: Inversione, Novis, Öfugt, Odwrócić, Omgekeerde, Sens Inverse, Terbalik, Baglæns, Umkehren & Zvrátit. Reverse翻译成中文"逆反差"，是一种有着200年历史的新潮字体风格！

jåçéñöû

1234567890

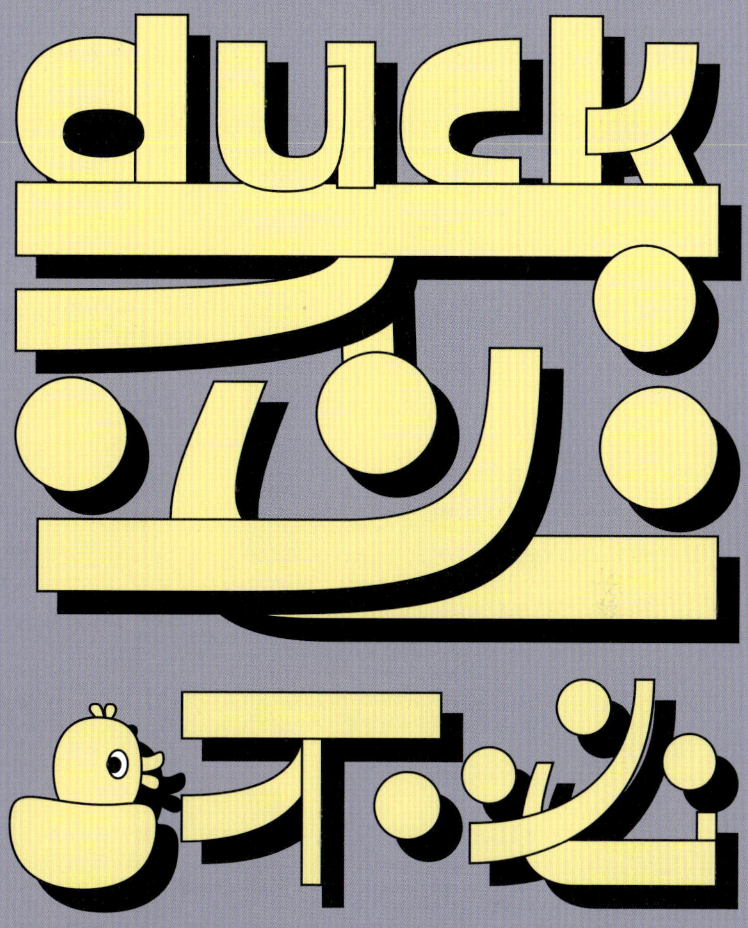

Inspired by the course, the designer found that such reverse designs were largely applied to the artistic calligraphy on the covers of various books and advertising posters since the Republic of China, some of which were strikingly similar to *RVS Basic*. The reverse-contrast Latin fonts have been used in visual design for 200 years. In this case, the seemingly trendy font is no more than a throwback.

哈哈哈哈哈哈
哈哈哈哈哈哈
哈哈哈哈哈哈
哈哈哈哈哈哈

注意高压电

「严是爱
松是害」

ATTENTION!

嘿嘿嘿嘿嘿嘿
嘿嘿嘿嘿嘿嘿
嘿嘿嘿嘿嘿嘿
嘿嘿嘿嘿嘿嘿

哟 LOL!
哟 LOL!
哟 LOL!
哟 LOL!
哟 LOL!
哟 LOL!
哟 LOL!
哟 LOL!
哟 LOL!
哟 LOL!

火 + 少 = 炒

赤 + 赤 = 赫

25. BILLBOARD CHINA

Warring States Period (476-221 BC) witnessed feudal lords contending for supremacy, while China's electronic music is now ushering in the era of talents coming forth in large numbers. The type design of " 制霸 " (Zhi Ba) takes the form of Ding, an ancient cooking vessel with two loop handles and three or four legs. Despite different degrees of stretching and deformation, the typeface always presents a relatively stable and strong visual form, which also matches the dignified presence of Ding. "China Top Electronic" is a Chinese electronic music competition organized by Billboard China. With the theme of originating from the local and spreading over the world, it is dedicated to presenting the local characteristics of Chinese electronic music while possessing a globally readable vision in meaning and style.

TD: Cao Fan, Shen Hongrui
DA: Hoooly Design

BILLBOARD DANCE
ZYLO
BILLBOARD DANCE
STEVE ROCKS
BBD
中国电音
DANCE
CISSY
DANCE
BILLBOARD DANCE BILLBOARD DANCE

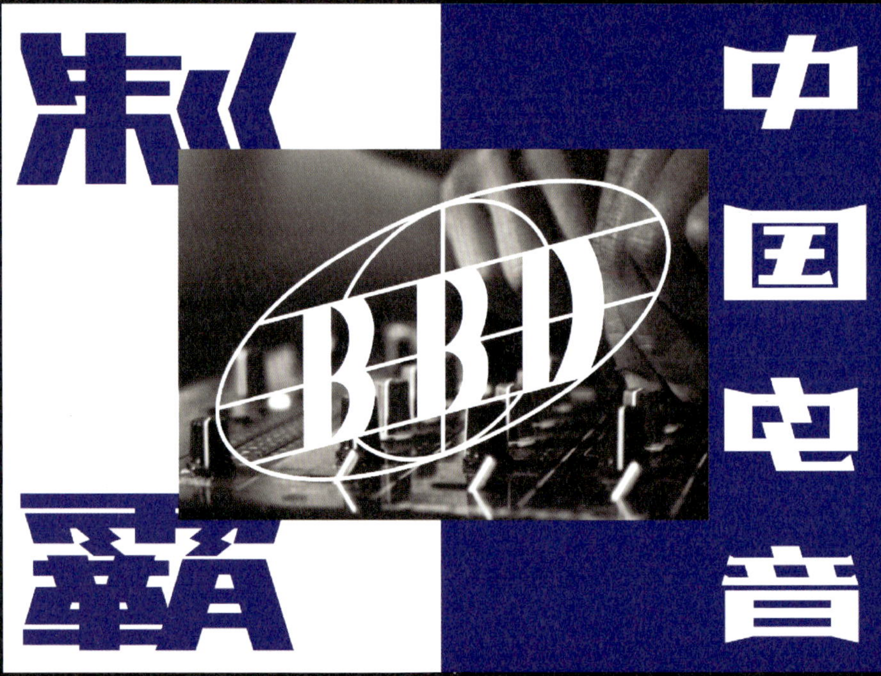

BBD

中国电音

中国电音
BBD

DANCE
JINACTION

BILLBOARD DANCE
中国电音
SPACE PLUS

국립극장 레퍼토리시즌
NATIONAL REPERTORY
SEASON 2019–2020
국립극장
National Theater of Korea
예매 및 문의 02-2280-4114 ntok.go.kr
국립극장
레퍼토리시즌
2019-2020

26. NTOK POSTER

The typeface is the key visual element of the poster of the NTOK[1] for its National Repertory Season 2019-2020. As a leading representative in the performing arts of Korea, the theatre has been running for 60 years and would put on a rich variety of performances, such as stage drama, traditional drama, dance, or symphony on every performance season.

TD: Jaemin Lee, Dawoon Jeon
DA: Studio fnt
CL: NTOK

① NTOK is short for the National Theatre of Korea.

국립극장 레퍼토리시즌
NATIONAL REPERTORY
SEASON 2019–2020

Inspired by the cut-outs originate from Matisse, a representative of the Beast Painting, the designer makes full use of such elements as petals and leaves in the poster, which are scattered freely and combined into fonts in a seemingly disordered manner. The “Dance” here is not just a kind of art form. By virtue of the theme, the designer expects to invoke deep feelings and pure desire, and have all of your senses engaged in the dance drama on the 70th anniversary of the theatre.

국립극장
레퍼토리시즌
NATIONAL
REPERTORY
SEASON
2019–2020
국립극장
레퍼토리시즌
2019-2020
7월 24일
티켓오픈
국립극장

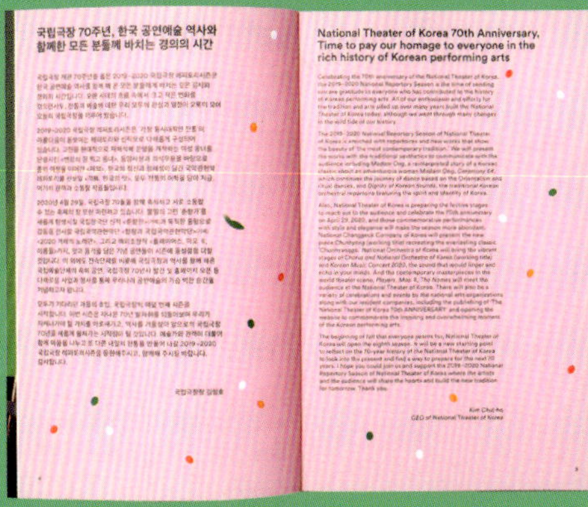
국립극장 70주년, 한국 공연예술 역사와 함께한 모든 분들께 바치는 경의의 시간
National Theater of Korea 70th Anniversary, Time to pay our homage to everyone in the rich history of Korean performing arts

국립무용단
National Dance Company of Korea

국립극장 레퍼토리시즌
NATIONAL REPERTORY SEASON 2019–2020

Part 4.
BETWEEN CONTRAST

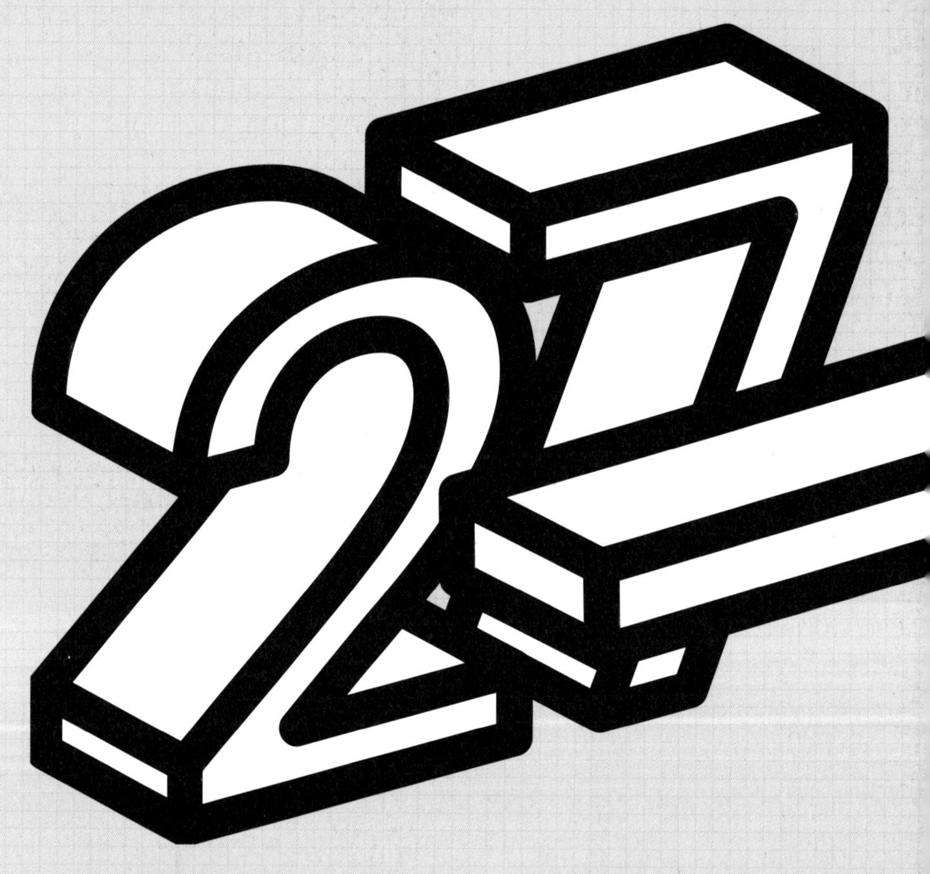

Design Language

Combination Exaggeration

27. 5UPER DISPLAY

5Uper Display is an experimental modular typeface in which each letter is made up of repeating shapes to create the structure of each letter-form. Characterized by the sharp pointed edge and the rounded, curved strokes that make distinct contrast, the typeface boasts an overall intimidating aesthetics with an unfamiliar twist. Putting aside readability, the designer is dedicated to developing the most visually impressive and unique typeface ever seen with the fewest forms.

TD: Ash Lane

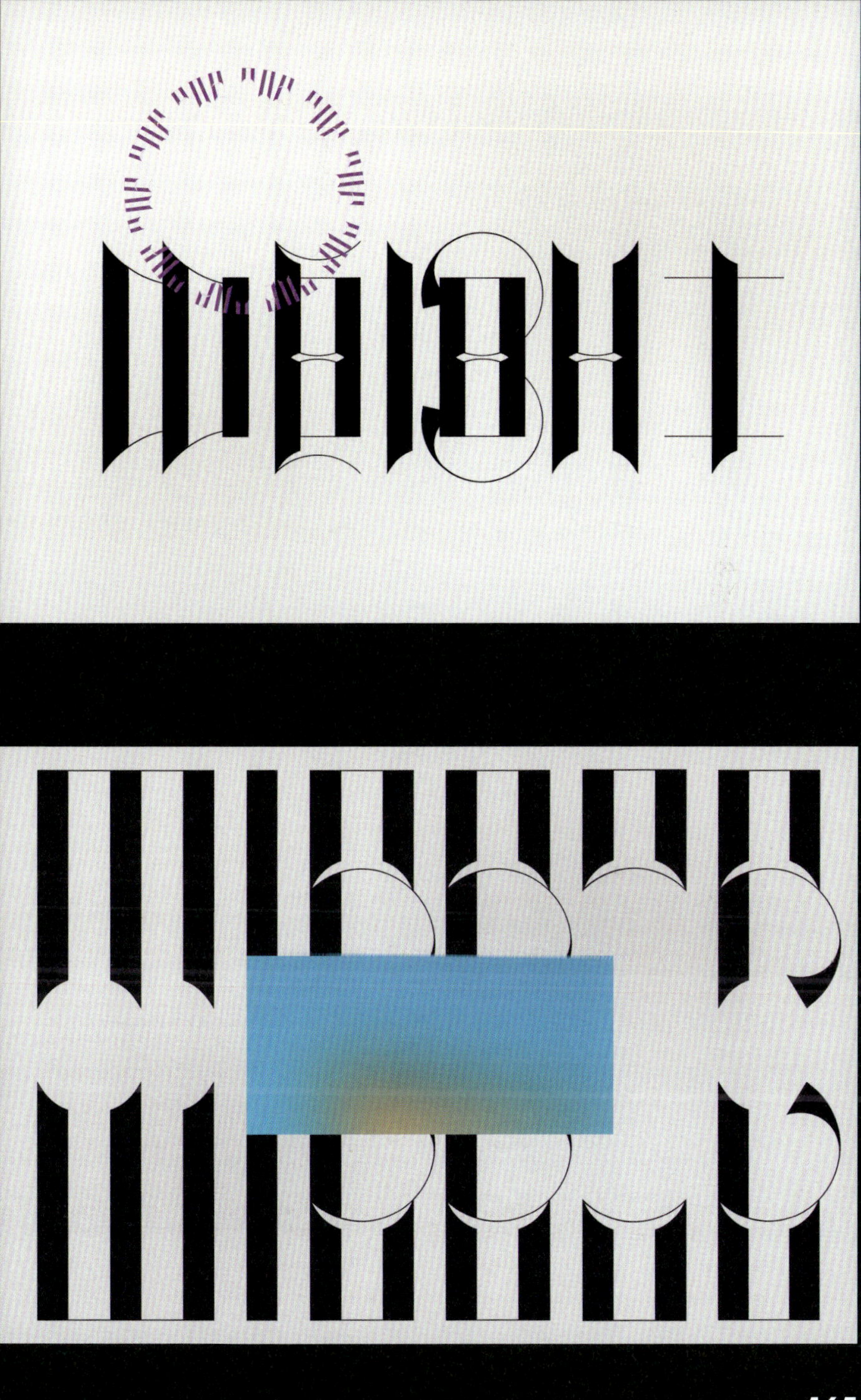

Fax back Jim's Gwyneth Paltrow video quiz Lawbooks forgave John Quincy Adams, sixth prez—Queen Elizabeth's major fox.

Nikolas Type
Düsseldorfer Str.68
51063 Cologne, DE
+49174 44 33 911

28. COSI AZURE

Cosi Azure is a typeface in sharp contrast to *Cosi Times*. The inspiration comes from the natural landscape and imposing manner of the Mediterranean islands of Sardinia and Corsica. The delicately flexible decorative serifs are counterposied with bolder and wilder chunks, evoking the sweet air, pointed peaks and the soothing sound of the sea.

Cosi Azure blends harmonic and erratic undertones in its form. It is a typeface born out of personal life experience.

TD: Nikolas Wrobel
F: Nikolas Type

ABCDEFG
HIJKLMNO
PQRSTUV
WXYZ123
4567890(!?)

FAN
TASY

COSI
AZZURE

FOAM MAGAZINE

MAKE ME FALL IN LOVE WITH THE (MUSIC)

foam
international photography magazine
PHOTOGRAPHY
MAGAZINE
OF THE YEAR.
AGAIN!
— Lucie Award
20
YOUNG ARTISTS
SHAPING THE FUTURE
OF PHOTOGRAPHY
TALENT

MO-
DU-
LAR

29. KREIS

Kreis is a modular typeface with a strikingly modern design inspired by the form of the old school CD. It consists of three simple modules with the roots in square and circle shapes. The letters are in a geometric typographic patterns while ensuring high readability. *Kreis* supports basic Cyrillic and Latin.

TD: Katerina Korolevtseva

KREIS

MODULAR

FONT

КРАЙС

МОДУЛЬНИЙ

ШРИФТ

EVERY

FLOWER

MUST GROW

THROUGH

DIRT

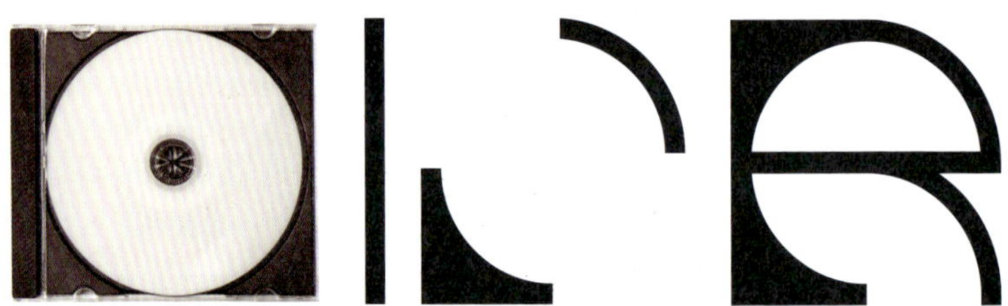

ABCDEFGHIJK
LMNOPQRSTUV
WXYZ

АБВГҐДЕЁЄЖЗ
ІЇИЙКЛМНОП Р
СТУФХЦЧШЩЬЫ
ЪЭЮЯ

0123456789

ACEEEFFFGIK
NOQRRTYYДЖ
ЁЁЁЇЛЛЯ

MODULAR TYPEFACE
MO
PE
FA
CE
KREIS

MODULAR TYPEFACE

MODULAR TYPEFACE

20

30. MISTO

Misto is a free reverse-contrast font, inspired by Slavutych, Ukraine's youngest city, which was born after the Chernobyl explosion. The city is filled with low scale, five-storey houses, distinctive postmodern architecture, and tall pine trees. Unlike the metropolis, it is a contemporary utopia and a small oasis of verdancy and tranquility.

Misto is a blend of the architectural styles in eight regions of the former Soviet Union. It features the lively annotations and symbols with rhythm, the ballpoint at the tail of strokes, the elliptical low oblong counters parts, and the interesting contrast among the clear-cut thickness of strokes. The glyphs with imposing manner are reminiscent of the low and wide buildings in Slavutych. It mirrors the urban vitality. The annotations and symbols cited in the Slavutych Museum give a glimpse of the rich source of inspiration behind the font.

TD: Katerina Korolevtseva

MISTO FONT

ABCDEFGHIJKLMN
OPQRSTUVWXYZ

АБВГҐДЕЁЄЖЗИІЇ
ЙКЛМНОПРСТУФХ
ЦЧШЩЬЫЪЭЮЯ

0123456789

– — ( ) , . ' : ; " " - + _ = # / % \ © ~
? ! * [ ] ‰ & « » ‹ › " @ № ✷ $ €

ККУЙЖЛЪRQ

Designed to promote local tourism and bring vigor to the city, the font shows great potential in shaping cultural life.

Misto is ideal for headings, including logos, brand vision, website design, packaging, and posters. It is unveiled in both Cyrillic and Latin. The designer hopes to contribute to the development of modern Cyrillic typefaces.

THIS
CITY
MAKES
ME
FALL
IN
LOVE

"FOR THOSE WHO ARE LOST,
THERE WILL ALWAYS BE CITIES
THAT FEEL LIKE HOME."

Simon Van Booy

31. FUN & FANCY FONT

The "36 Days of Type" is a design project that has been running on social media for 7 years. The designers are required to release 26 letters and 10 numerical symbols within 36 days. Designers participated in the event spontaneously, aiming to break with tradition and inspire creativity by exchanges.

The bold coloring is incorporated into the font to make a sharp contrast in shape and proportion. The roughness and subtlety of the strokes mix well. The designer hopes to encourage others to break the rules and create something unique.

TD: Adriana Guillén

wów
wów
wów

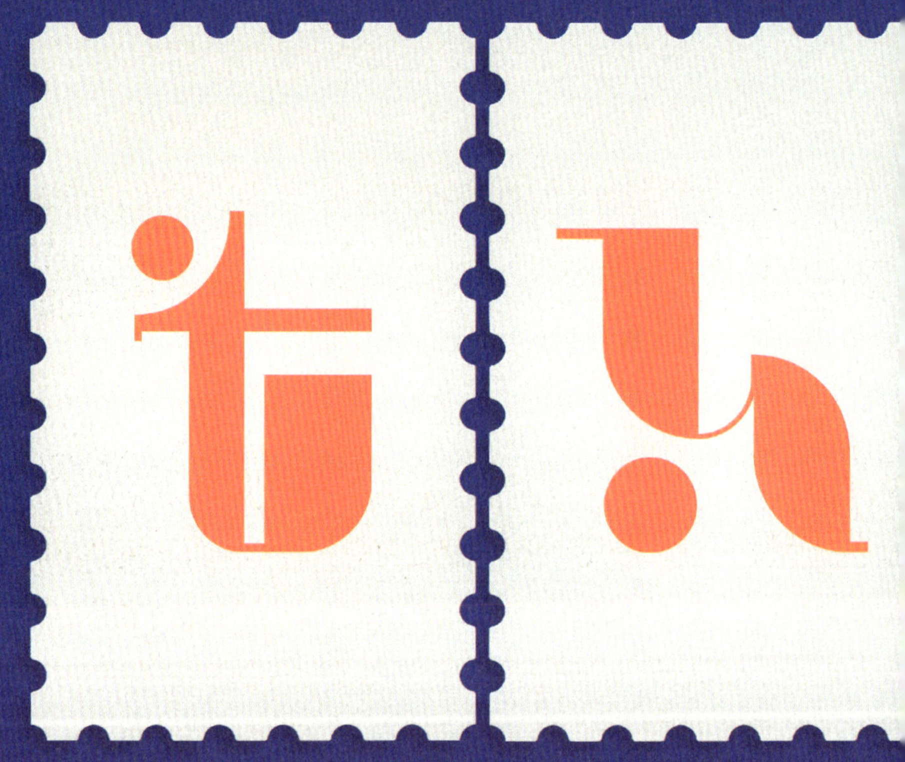

32. DAZE DISPLAY

Daze Display is a font with sharp contrast, especially in line, weight, and the difference between straight line and curved line.

It is designed for the display of larger-size types, emphasizing that the shapes of the letters appear as simple as possible, and balancing the features of geometric lines and the curved lines. The major challenges in the process of creating types are the shade working with a square grid. The designer prefers the way the font challenges readability and explores the possibility of fonts as the elements of texture.

TD: Gemma Mahoney, Si Billam

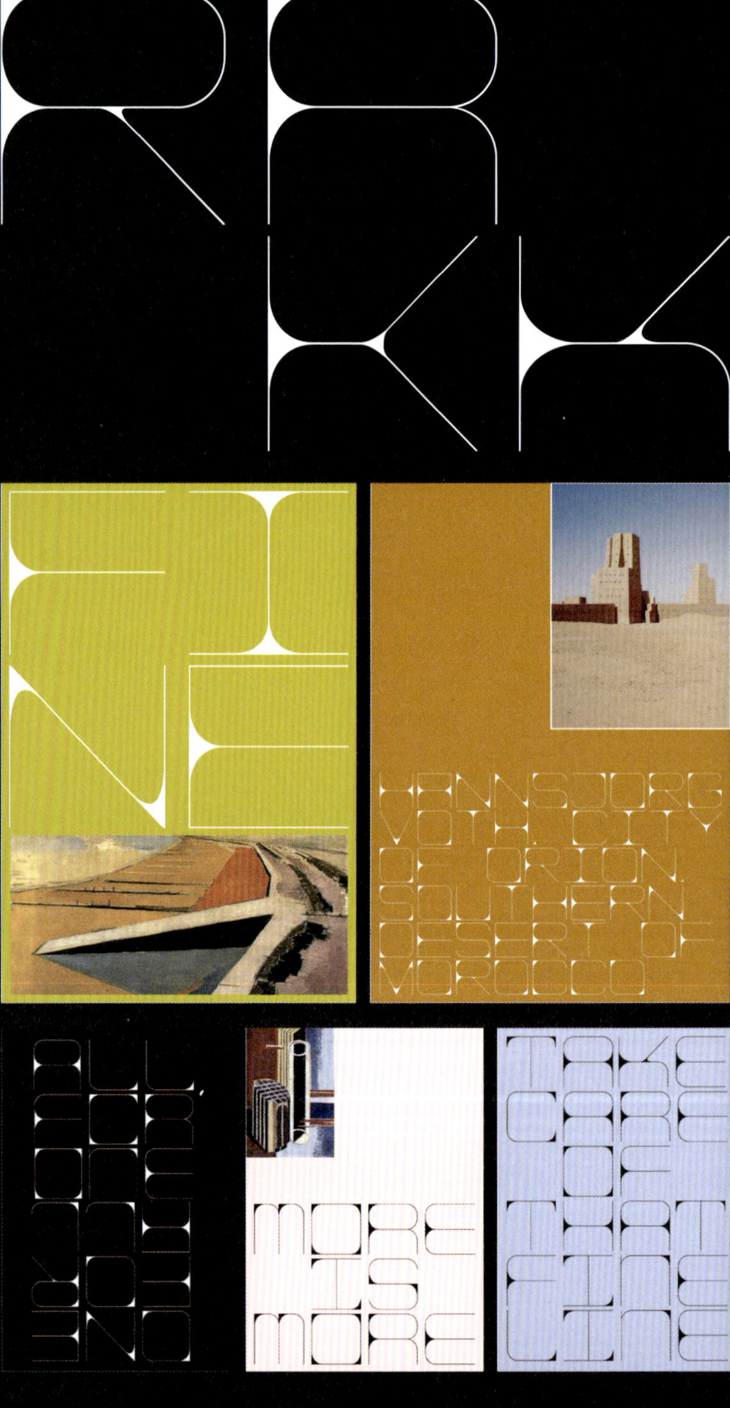
HANNSJORG
VOTH, CITY
OF ORION,
SOUTHERN
DESERT OF
MOROCCO
MORE
IS
MORE

IN THE
RECK–
LESS

33. BERLIN

The design concept of the album Berlin is out of the attempt of the singer Zhang Xiaohou to explore the world of music personally for the first time. It spans space and time, and makes interpersonal exploration, releasing the hidden part of the self. *Berlin* is a font designed for the album. By means of the structural fragmentation, reorganization, and texture mapping, it presents the process as *Berlin* is reorganized, which makes the known self expand and extend to the unknown. The visual elements intersperse with the type themes, taking on the album concept of the unknown and exploration.

TD&D: Cao Fan, Shen Hongrui
DA: Hoooly Design

BERLIN
BERLIN
BERLIN
BERLIN
BERLIN
ERLIN
BERLIN

BERLIN
BERLIN
BERLIN
BERLIN
BERLIN
柏
林

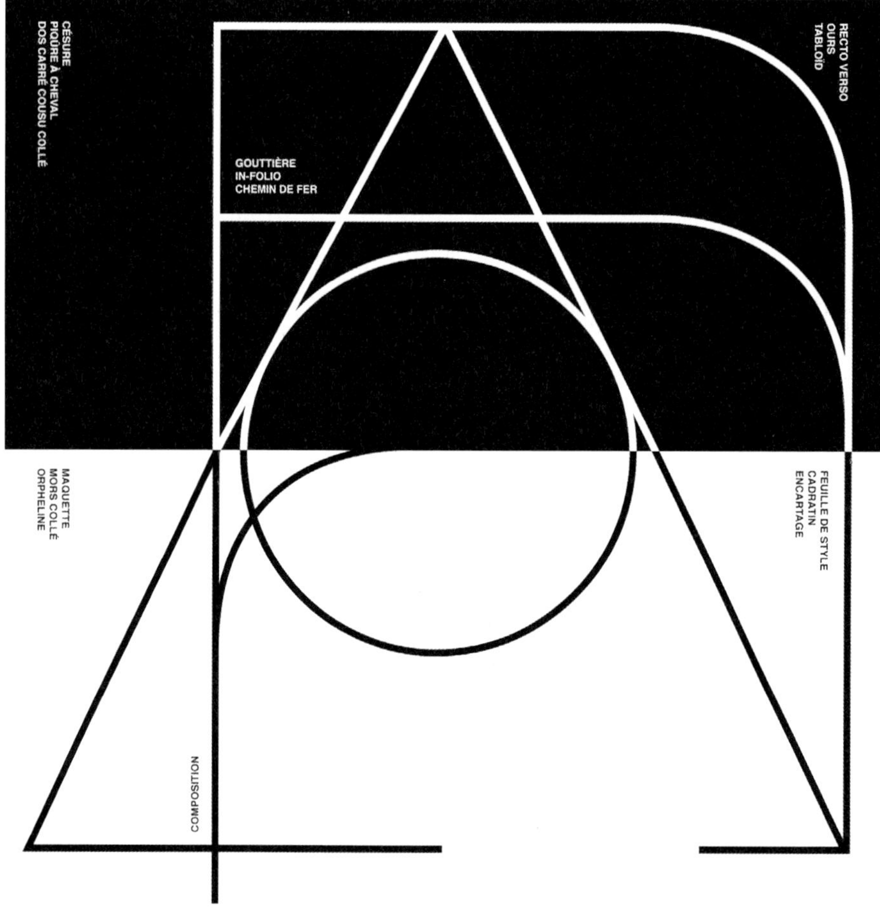
CÉSURE
PIQÛRE À CHEVAL
DOS CARRÉ COUSU COLLÉ
GOUTTIÈRE
IN-FOLIO
CHEMIN DE FER
RECTO VERSO
OURS
TABLOÏD
MAQUETTE
MORS COLLÉ
ORPHELINE
FEUILLE DE STYLE
CADRATIN
ENCARTAGE
COMPOSITION

34. SCREEN SPLASH

Designers of My Name is Wendy teamed up with visual artist Rus Khasanov to create the splash screen for Adobe InDesign CC 2018. The designers first extracted the core competence of the team by freehand sketching and determined the direction of the project. In addition, they thought it was necessary to combine their differences to create a contrasting artwork since it could bring a new visual experience. The Studio designed geometric shapes with concise lines, while Rus took abstract, vibrant pictures of floating pigments.

DA: My Name is Wendy
A: Rus Khasanov
CL: Adobe

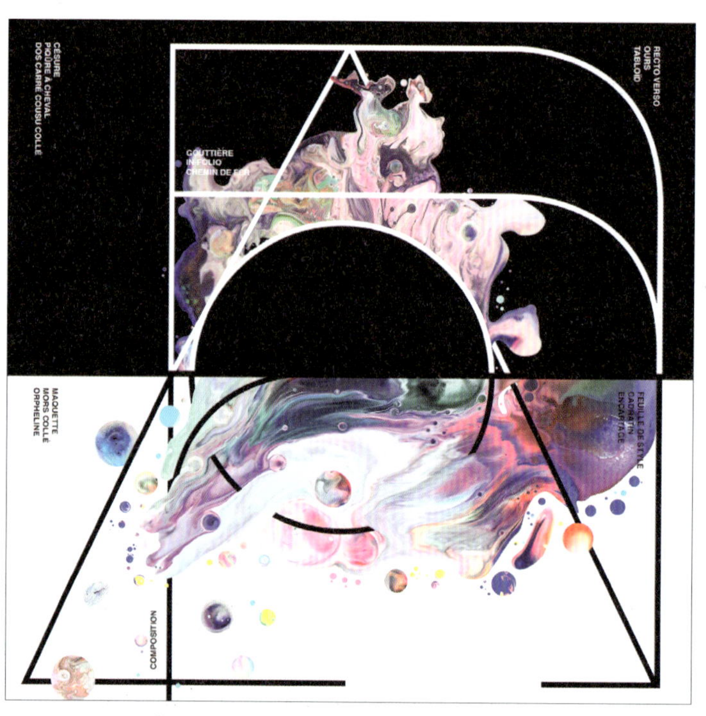
RECTO VERSO
OURS
TABLOÏD
CÉSURE
PIQÛRE À CHEVAL
DOS CARRÉ COUSU COLLÉ
MAQUETTE
MORS COLLÉ
ORPHELINE
COMPOSITION

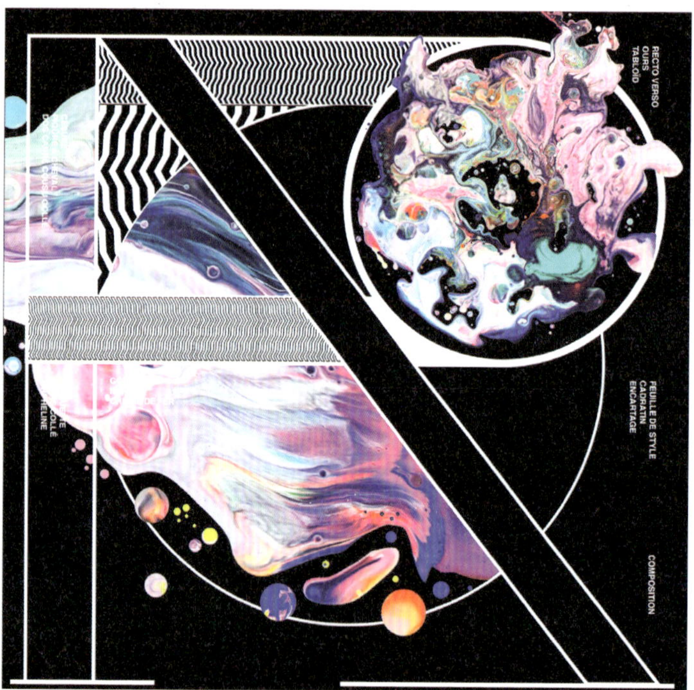
RECTO VERSO
OURS
TABLOÏD
FEUILLE DE STYLE
CADRATIN
ENCARTAGE
COMPOSITION

Part 5.
BIZARRE

Design Language

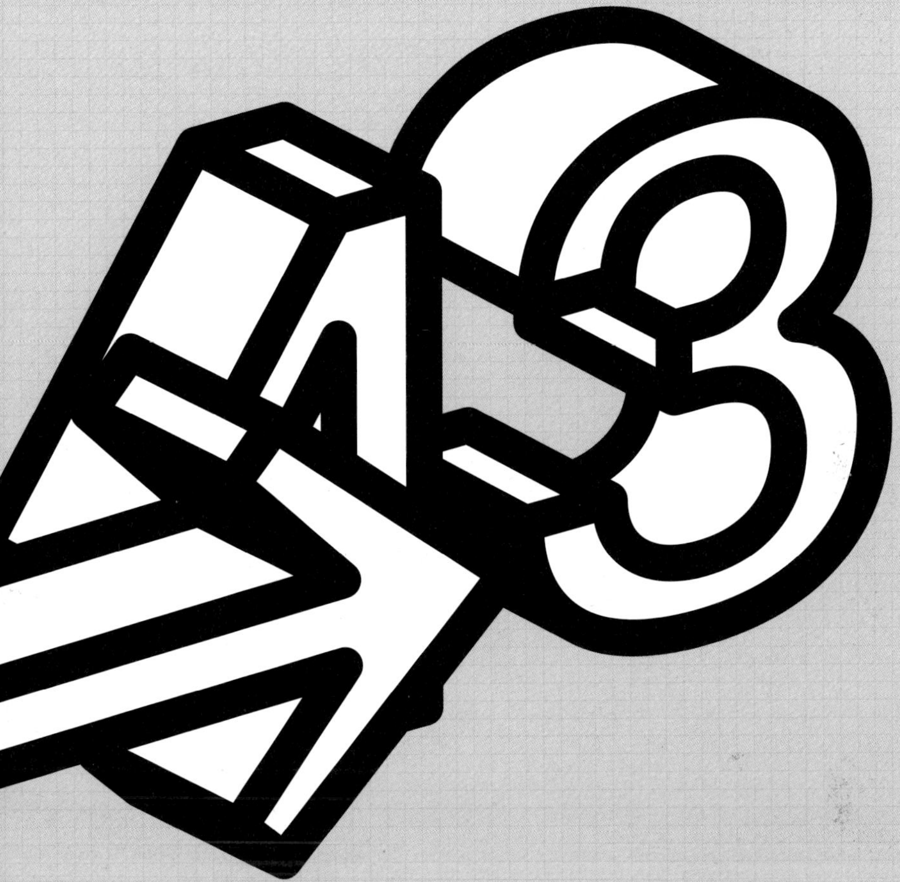

35. LOBULAR

Lobular is a font that looks like the cross-section of the intestinal tube cut and sliced. It mimics the features of ink trap with the joints connected by the smooth short and straight lines. As the only flat parts of the font, the joints are designed only to meet the requirements of visual structure, rather than to impede the diffusion. The font shape is also reminiscent of the bubble type used in street graffiti.

TD: Ariel Maritn Pérez

REGULAR

72 PTS

CLOSTRIDIUM SPOROGENS

48 PTS

GUTES SAUERKRAUT

24 PTS

DAVID EXIGE PLAZO FIJO, EMBARQUE TRUCHAS Y NIÑOS A NEW YORK.

18 PTS

LES QUELQUE 150 ESPÈCES DE BACILLES SPORULÉS ANAÉROBIES APPARTENANT AU GENRE CLOSTRIDIUM SONT DES GERMES SAPROPHYTES TELLURIQUES INTERVENANT DANS LA PUTRÉFACTION DES DÉCHETS ORGANIQUES. ILS PEUVENT AUSSISE TROUVER EN COMMENSAUX DE LA FLORE INTESTINALE, SURTOUT CHEZ LES HERBIVORES MAIS ÉGALEMENT CHEZ L'HOMME.

TOTALLY VEGAN

AND ROUNDILICIOUS

ABCDEFGHIJKLMNOP

QRSTUVWXYZ

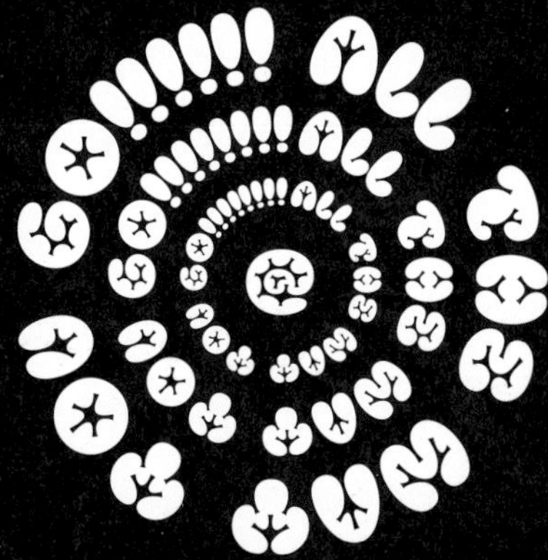

THE QUICK BROWN
FOX JUMPS OVER
THE LAZY SAUSAGE

LOBULAR RESEARCH FACILITIES™

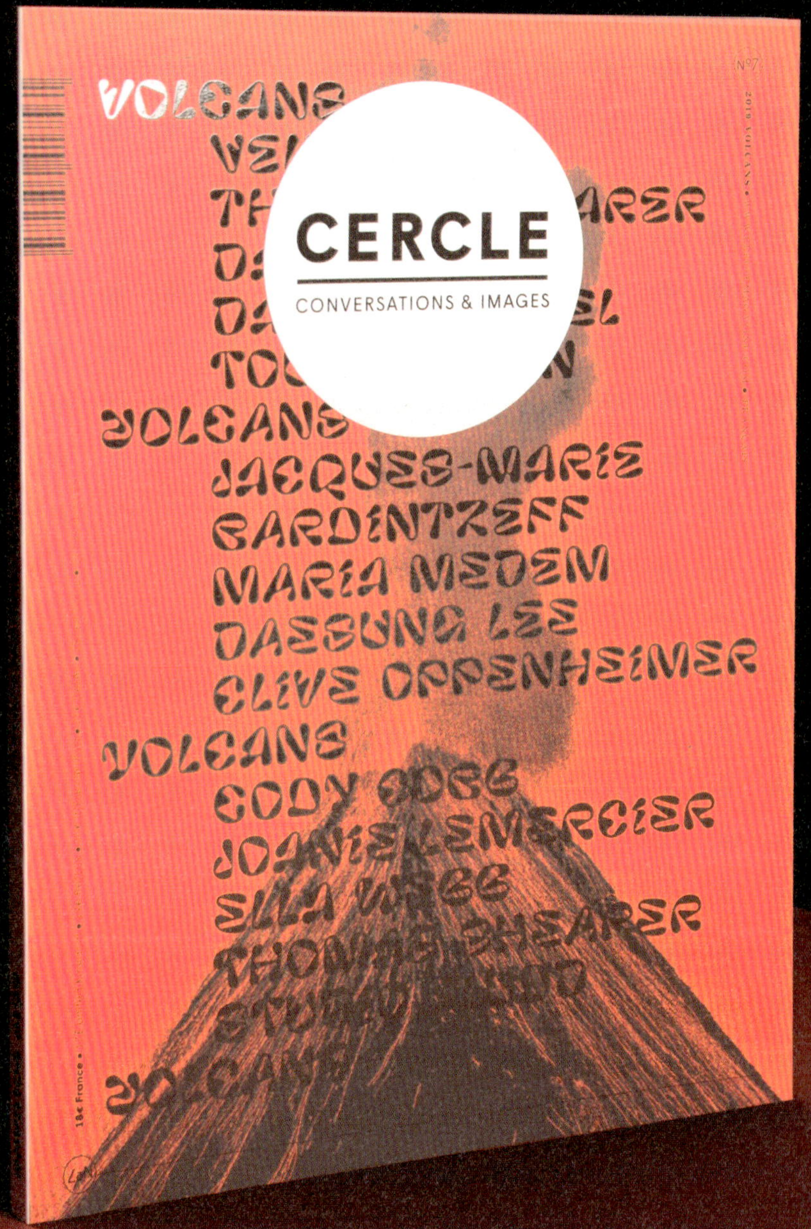
N°7
VOLCANS
CERCLE
CONVERSATIONS & IMAGES
VOLCANS
JACQUES-MARIE
BARDINTZEFF
MARIA MEDEM
DAESUNG LEE
CLIVE OPPENHEIMER
VOLCANS
18€ France

36. PILOWLAVA

The typeface *Pilowlava* takes its name from pillow lava, a phenomenon which arises after the volcanic lava condenses rapidly into the water when it cools with water. It is composed of irregular spheres overlaying one over another with the vitreous outer layer. It resembles a round pillow, hence its name.

The font created originally by two designers in one stretch, draws inspiration from pillow-shaped lava, mimicking the effect of a compass submerged inside. It seeks a balance between intense energy and straightforward geometry.

TD: Anton Moglia, Jérémy Landes
F: Velvetyne Type Foundry

PILOWLAVA

JÉRÉMY LANDES
*
STUDIO TRIPLE

ANTON MORLIA
*
MAOUS STUDIO

VELVETYNE TYPE FOUNDRY

*

Pilowlava

ABCDEFGHIJKLMN
OPQRSTVWXYZÁĂÂÃ
ÄÀĀĄÅÃÆĆČÇĊĐĎĐÉĚ
ÊËĖÈĒĘĞĢĠĦÍÎÏÌĪĶĹĽŁŃŇ
ŅŊÑÓÔÖÒŐŌØÕŒÞŔŘŖŚŠ
ŞȘŦŤŢȚÚÛÜÙŰŪŲŮẂŴ
ẄẀÝŶŸỲŹŽŻ$€ß
№1234567890
&°!¿?!@%ß'
{([«*»])}
‘’“,-./••”’

*

The font is mainly derived from the flexible strokes of handwriting. The designer gets inspiration from handwriting and graffiti. The subtle discontinuity brings up the character of coupling hardness with softness and produces vacillating, fluctuating typographic color. Some curves are embodied by the almost-mathematical tension of its curves. Under a hardened crust frame, *Pilowlava* awaits the smallest temperature rise to recover its viscosity. The alternate shapes of certains letters play out these thermic accidents and raise the temperature of the text.

La Planete Sauvage
D: Angello Torres

Club Pinte
D: Céliane Nouzet

The poster is designed for the TWL Winter Solstice Banquet 2019. The designer creates three Chinese characters in line with the characteristics of *Pilowlava* while retaining the visual style of the original Latin.

Poster for the Winter Solstice Banquet 2019
D: Jaemin Lee
CL: TWL Shop

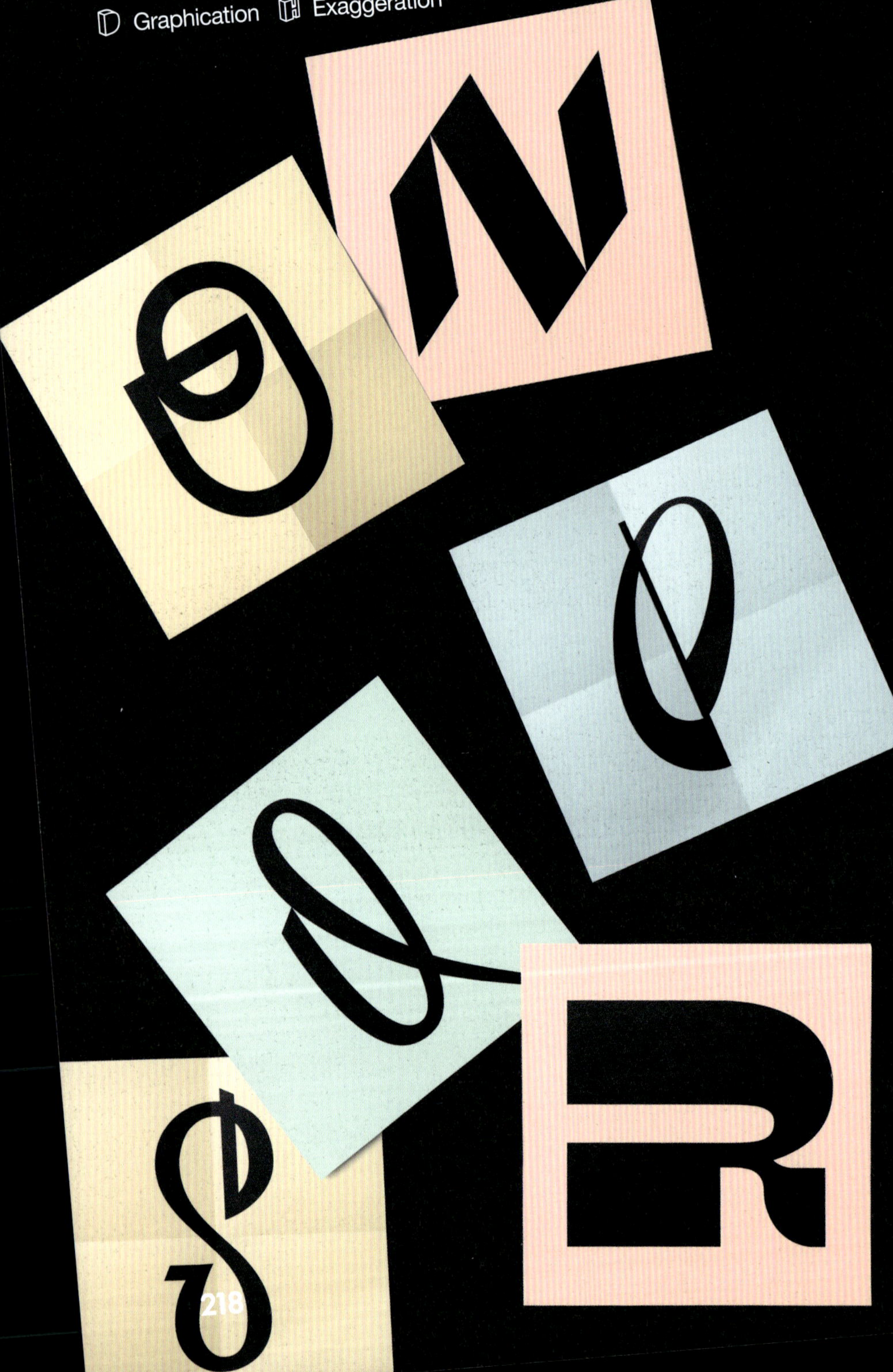

37. TYPOGRAPHY EXPERIMENT CHALLENGE

The designer draws a number of pencil sketches to create the typeface, highlighting the specific parts of each font and vectorizing the most interesting ones from those sketches. The typeface is like scattered colored pencil, with each letter born with a unique and novel idea.

TD: Nastya Novikova

38. ALPHABET

Creating for the "36 Days of Type", the designer stuck to the key point of keeping all the letters in tune without losing the uniqueness.

The designer wanted to create a playful typeface. For him/her it was important to exaggerate some parts of each letter enough to personify them, but keeping the traditional weights in its structure so they would be recognisable at the first glance.

TD: Carmen Nácher

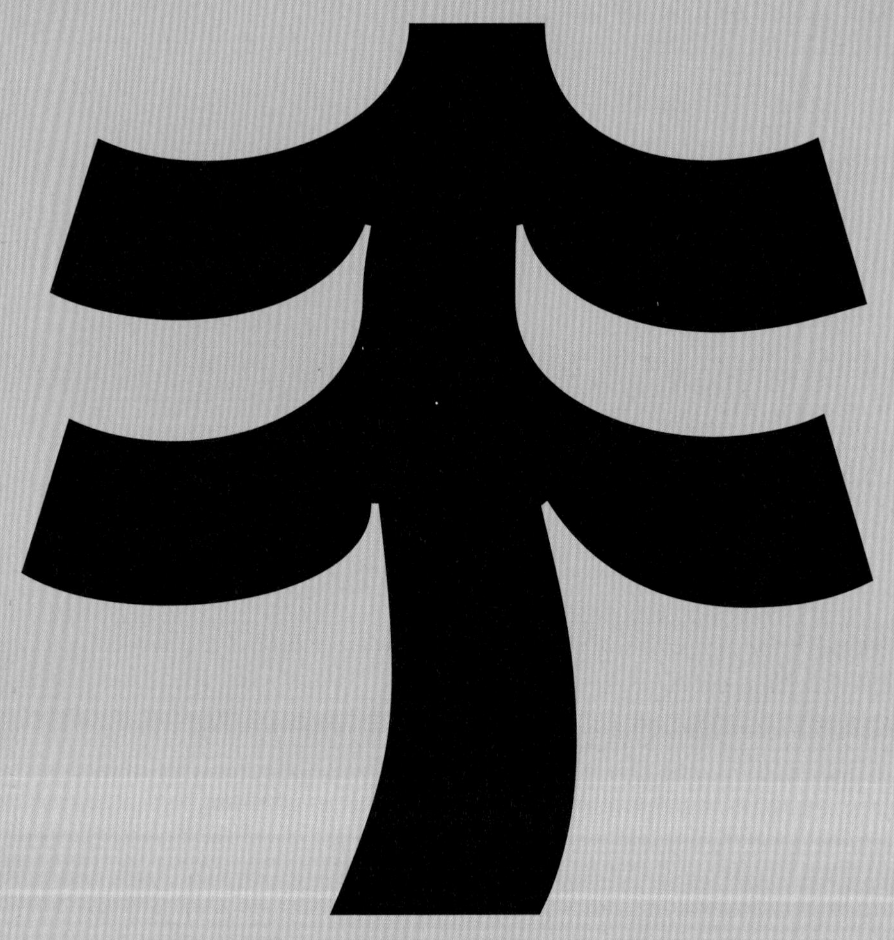

39. BRASSIA

Brassia, which means orchid, is reminiscent of peculiar-looking plants. It implies a timeless view of the nature of Solarpunk, the early 21st-century sci-fi aesthetic inspired by the Art Nouveau movement. In fact, some letters of *Brassia* have the potential for sustainable evolution, reflecting that the transformation and metamorphosis, including physical and mental states of human that we experience through our lives.

The most amazing part of this font is that you may never know what the next letter is going to look like by looking at one letter alone.

TD: Ariel Martín Pérez

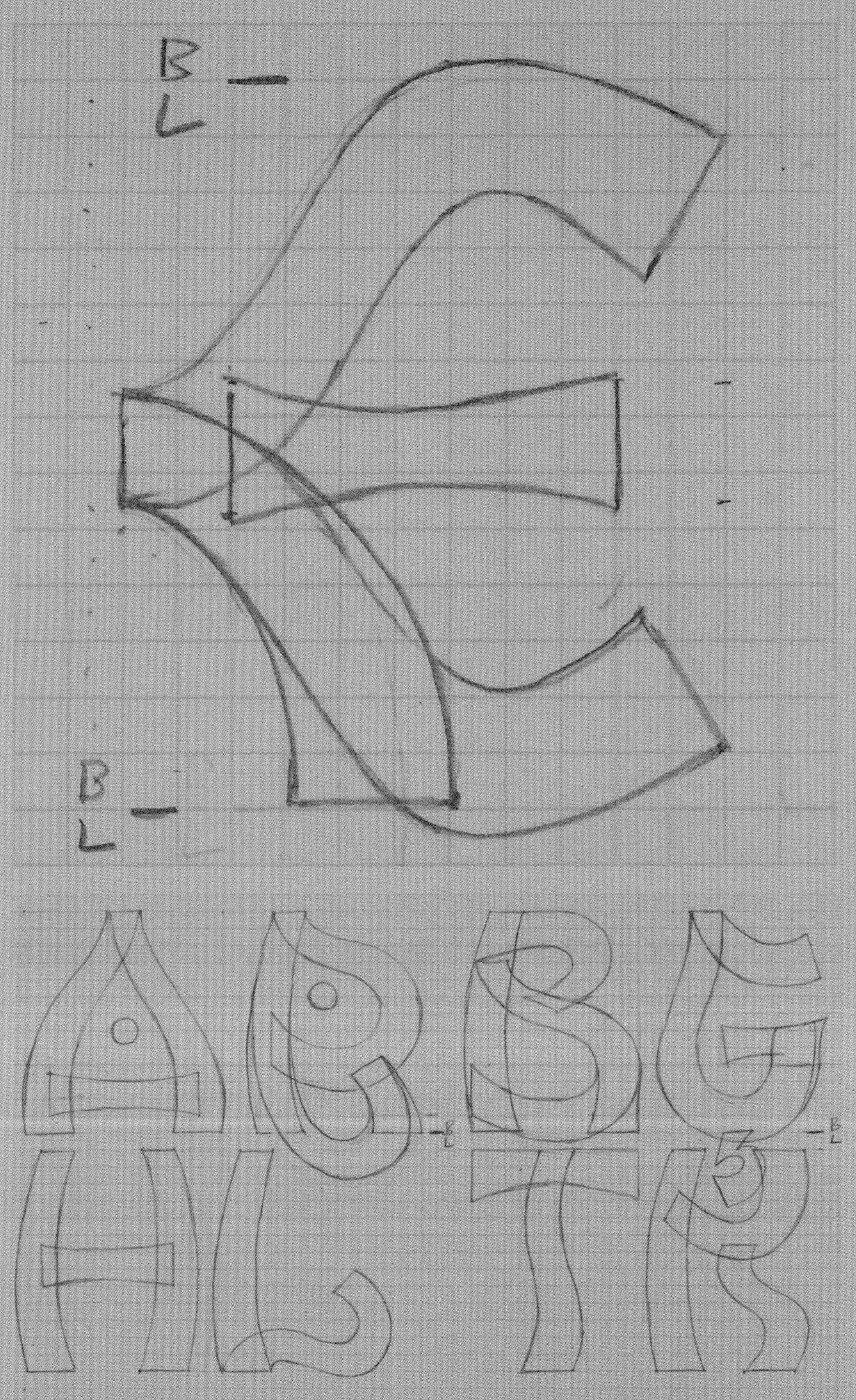
B
L
B
L

72 PTS

VERNACULAR ÆSTHETICS

48 PTS

BRUXELLES-MIDI

24 PTS

JOVE XEF, PORTI WHISKY AMB QUINZE GLAÇONS D'HIDROGEN, COI!

18 PTS

SOLARPUNK IS A MOVEMENT THAT ENCOURAGES OPTIMISTIC ENVISIONINGS OF THE FUTURE IN LIGHT OF PRESENT ENVIRONMENTAL CONCERNS, SUCH AS CLIMATE CHANGE AND POLLUTION, AS WELL AS SOCIAL INEQUALITY. SOLARPUNK ENCOMPASSES A MULTITUDE OF MEDIA SUCH AS LITERATURE, ART, ARCHITECTURE, FASHION, MUSIC, AND GAMES.

SNOT

40. SNOT

A font that children love should be rather entertaining. The designer starts from the shape and material that interest him most and draws inspiration from three things that arouse his strong memory of childhood. The first is that when he was a child, he happened to see a strange and exaggerated font on vacation in Poland (for a Scandinavian who upholds minimalist tradition, it is worthwhile to ruminate over these fonts). The second is his feeling when watching the green seriflux change shape, the last is a grotesque figure named Gogo's.

TD&D: Søren Steenstrup Højen
DA: Sunfried Studio

BØRN
SPISER
SNOT

FRUGT
ER IKKE
SLIK

NEVER GOAT TO BED
ENERGY DRINK
GOAT
MILK
250ML

THE PLANET OF THE
CREATIVE
STUDIO NAME PICTURE PRESENTS A PRODUCERS A FILM BY SCRIPT WRITER ACTOR ONE ACTOR TWO "MOVIE TITLE"
MUSIC BY THE MUSICIAN COSTUME DESIGNER DESIGNER NAME EDITED BY EDITOR NAME PRODUCTION DESIGNER DESIGNERS NAME DIRECTOR OF PHOTOGRAPHY CINEMATOGRAPHER
EXECUTIVE PRODUCER EX PRODUCER 1 EXPRODUCER 2 PRODUCED BY PRODUCER 1 PRODUCER 2 STORY BY STORY WRITER
SCREENPLAY BY SCREEN WRITER DIRECTED BY DIRECTOR NAME

41. GAFA

Gafa Online Degree Show 2020

"Circulation is a state of symbiosis, which transcends time and space and includes groups and individuals. It is both inclusive and open. It is a value 'community' that integrates individuality and commonness."The Mobius Ring takes such form. It creates a variety of complex cyclic structures even being twisted and establishes a system of magical form. Based on this structure, the three-dimensional visual image of the English abbreviation of Guangzhou Academy of Fine Arts "GAFA" is created after variation.

TD&D: Tian Bo
DA: TEN BUTTONS
CL: Guangzhou Academy of Fine Arts

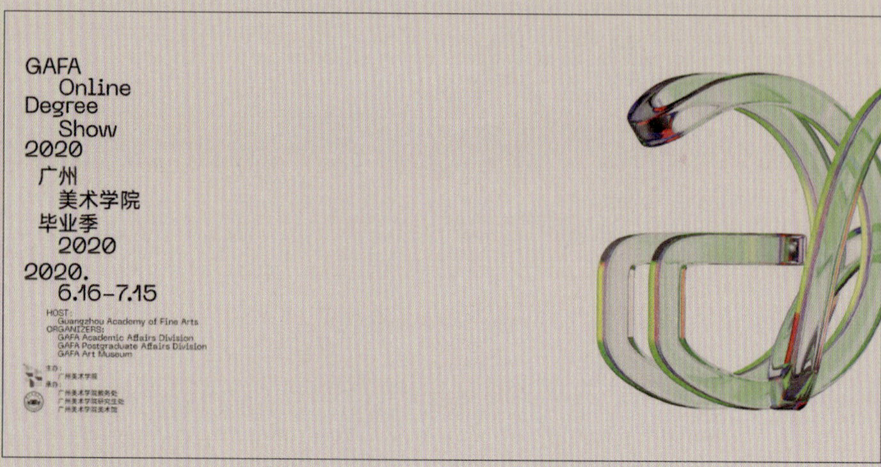
GAFA
Online
Degree
Show
2020
广州
美术学院
毕业季
2020
2020.
6.16-7.15
HOST:
Guangzhou Academy of Fine Arts
ORGANIZERS:
GAFA Academic Affairs Division
GAFA Postgraduate Affairs Division
GAFA Art Museum

GAFA
Online
Degree
Show
2020
广州
美术学院
毕业季
2020
2020.
6.16-7.15
HOST:
Guangzhou Academy of Fine Arts
ORGANIZERS:
GAFA Academic Affairs Division
GAFA Postgraduate Affairs Division
GAFA Art Museum

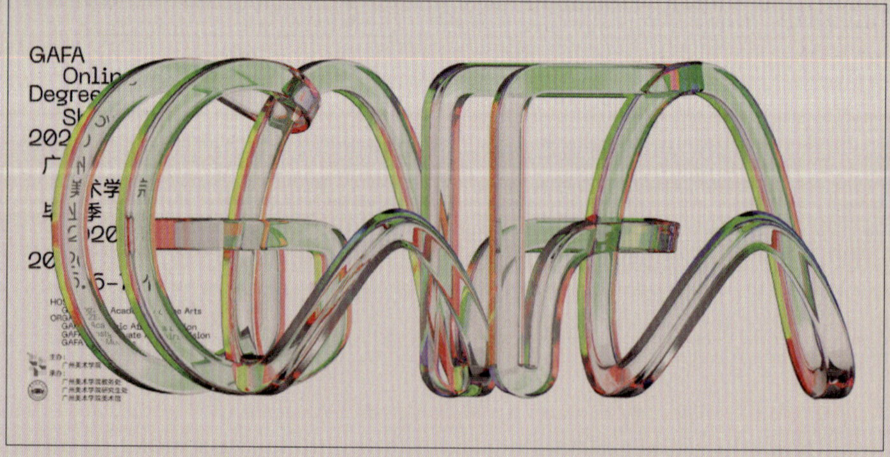
GAFA

Wireframe

Wireframe Model

Wireframe Rendering

In the three-dimensional space, the typeface has experienced the visual transformation from flat to three-dimension. The transparent material refracts the colorful dazzle light, and the rich colors of the light create more sense of mystery. The “G” and “A”, as well as the “F” and “A”, are superimposed on each other to create an optical illusion that interfered and merged, and the dynamic effects are presented to vividly show the youthfulness and playfulness of the design.

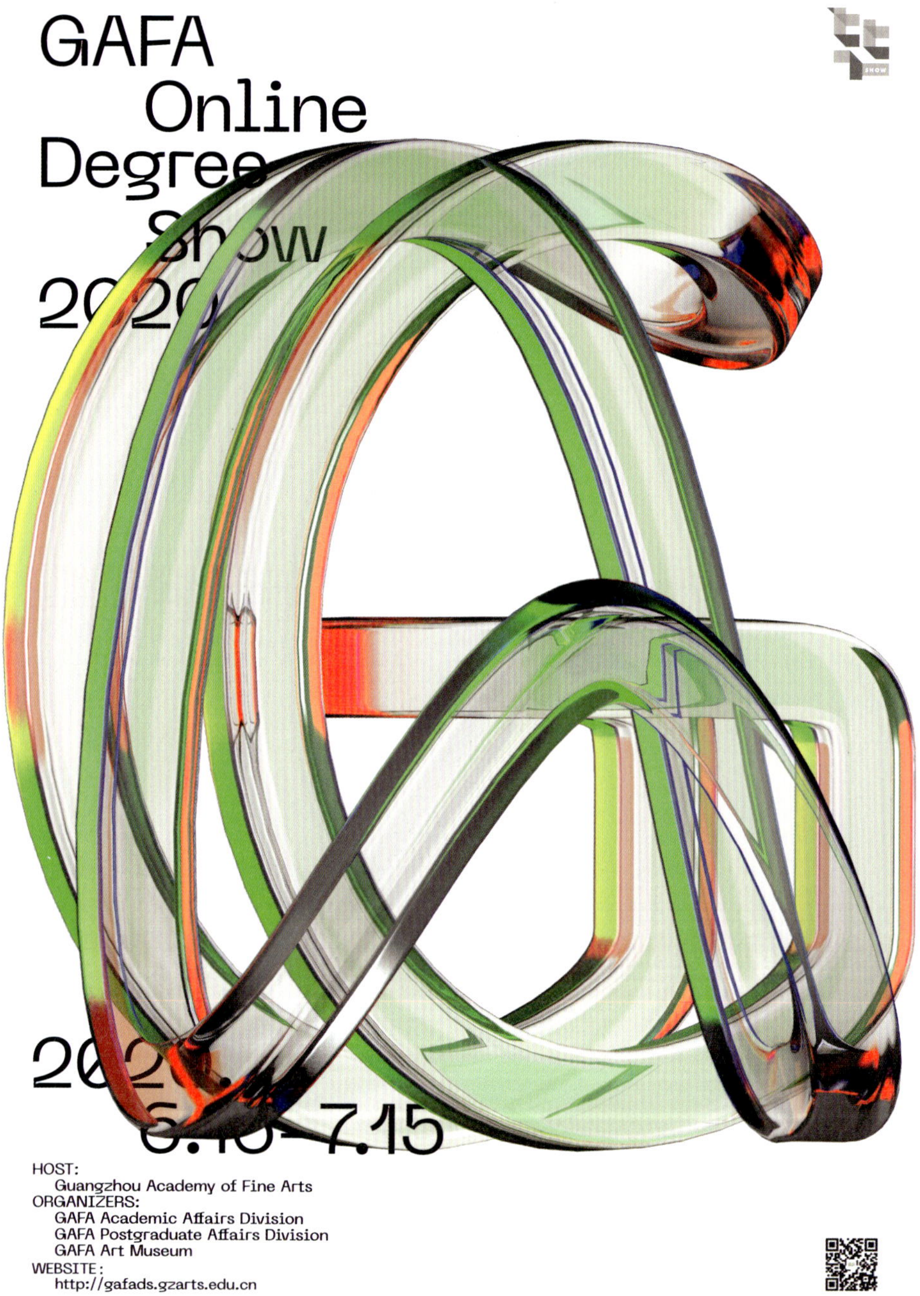

GAFA
Online
Degree
Show
2020

2020.
6.15–7.15

HOST:
Guangzhou Academy of Fine Arts
ORGANIZERS:
GAFA Academic Affairs Division
GAFA Postgraduate Affairs Division
GAFA Art Museum
WEBSITE:
http://gafads.gzarts.edu.cn

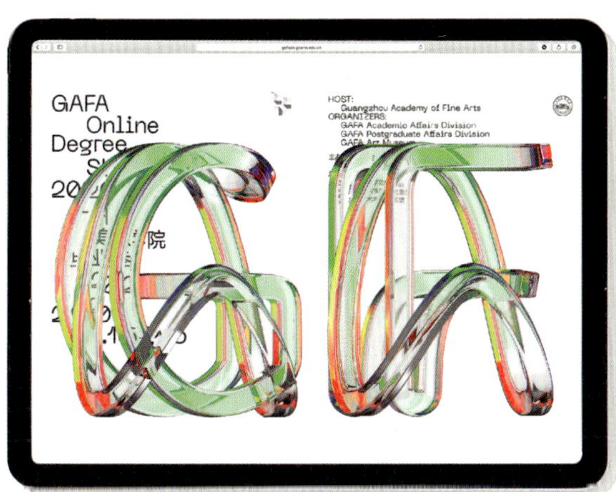

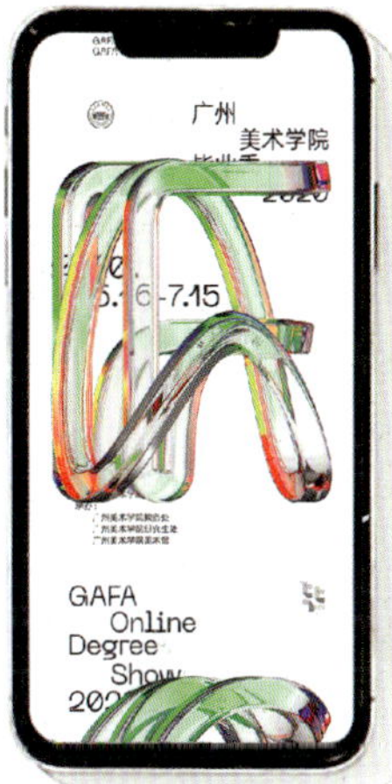

The visual identity of the degree show of GAFA is the interpretation of youth, which uses the then most avant-garde visual elements. The whole identity for the degree show includes websites, WeChat post, poster, handbag, badge, T-shirt, notebook, etc.

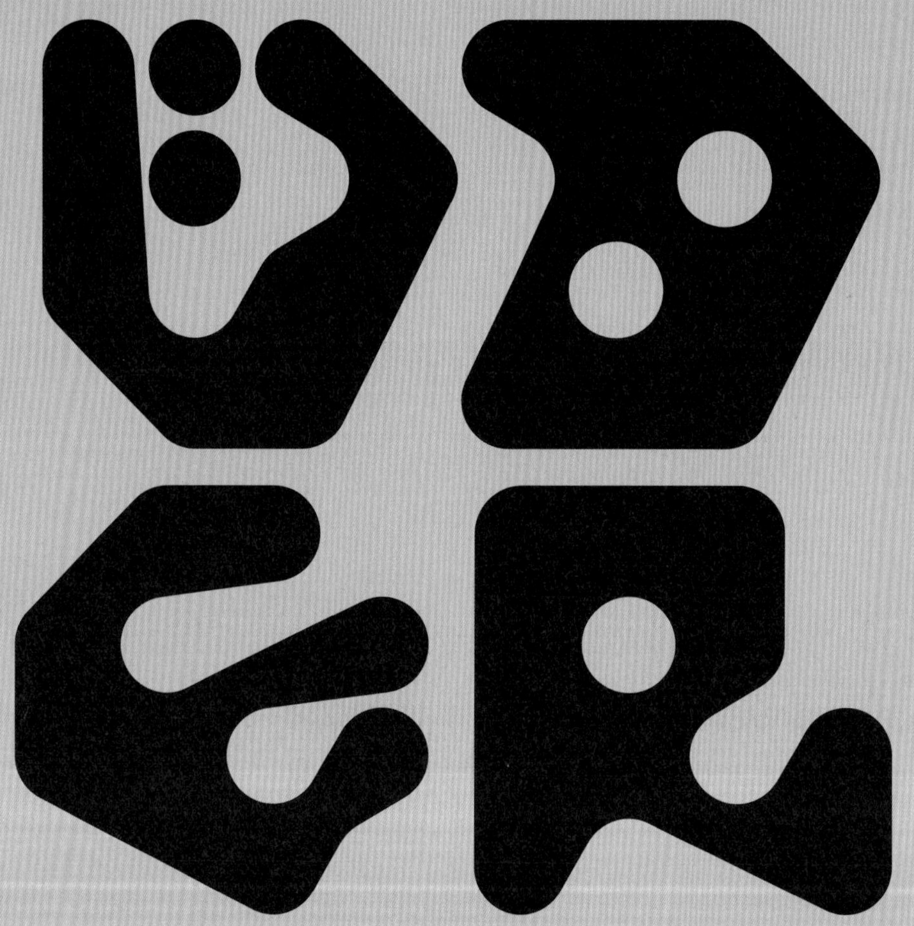

42. HOFMANN

As a tribute to the Swiss designer Armin Hofmann, the glyphs are designed based on a grid system created by Hofmann.

Hofmann is one of the leading figures in the International Typographic Style①. Many of his classic posters in the 1960s ushered in the Swiss Style whose influence still works currently. In addition to being a designer, Hofmann is very influential in design education.

TD: David Gobber
AD: NGUYENGOBBER

① The International Typographic Style, also known as the Swiss Style, flourishes after World War II. It adopts the grid as the design basis and uses a large quantity of sans serifs. It advocates simple and highly functional design with influence on this day.

VIRUS & BACTERIA

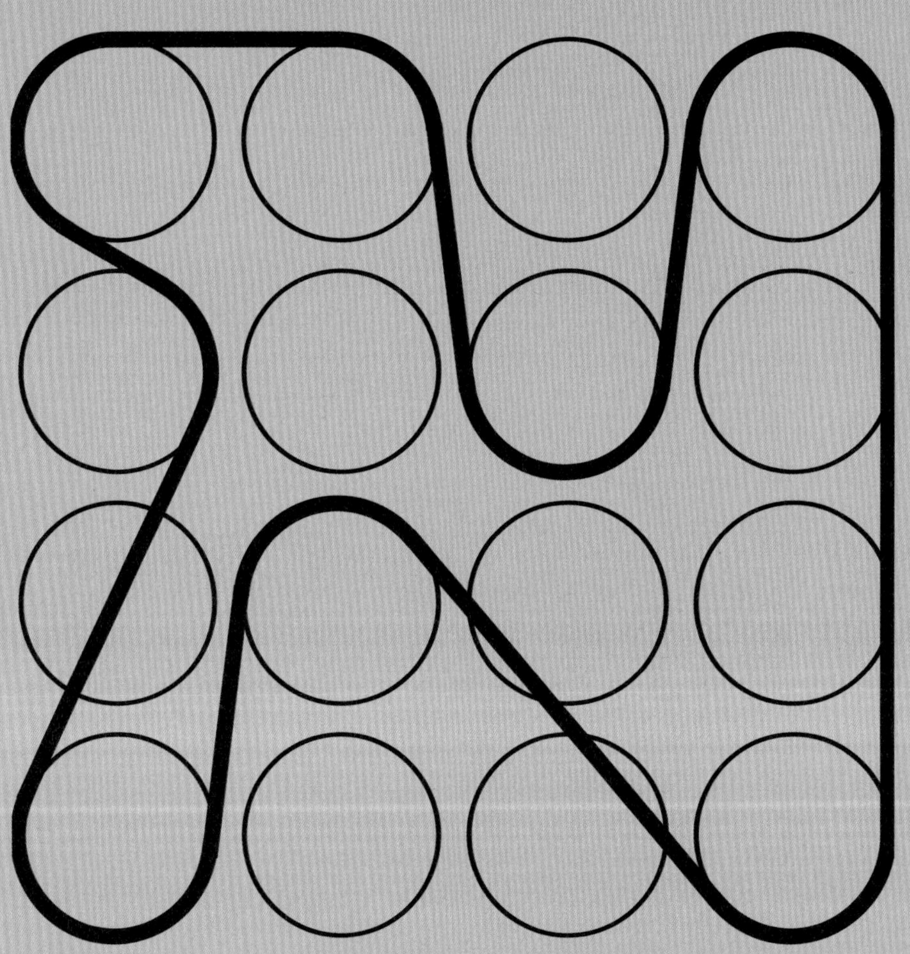

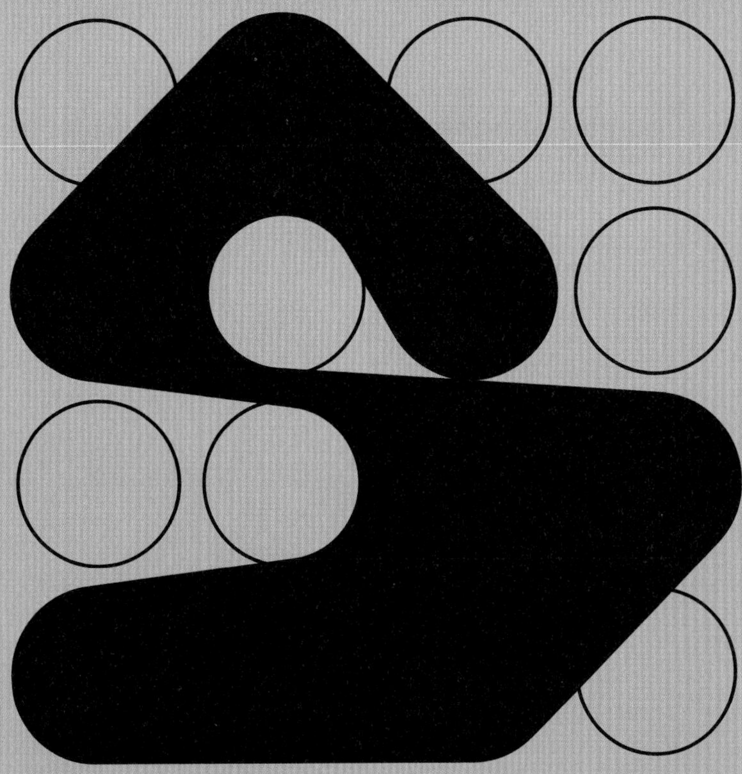

The designer mentions that a grid system is rarely applied in an original design but is more often used as an experimental tool to study visual design. Therefore, the typeface *Hofmann* probes into more possibilities with grid tools and challenges the limits of font design, to present the final product of a strong style.

Hofmann is not suitable for works that highlight readability as the primary premise. The typeface breaks many traditional frameworks to create surreal word marks which fit unconventional type posters and eye-catching headlines.

EXPE
RI
MEN
TAL

ARMIN HOFMANN (*1920) HAD HIS 100TH BIRTHDAY THIS YEAR!

HE IS WITHOUT ANY DOUBT ONE OF THE MOST INFLUENTIAL DESIGNERS FROM SWITZERLAND

43. DEMO

DESIGN IN MOTION FESTIVAL

An exciting new concept devised by Studio Dumbar in partnership with Exterion Media NL, the inaugural DEMO① festival took place on 7 November 2019 at Amsterdam Central station. The first festival of its kind, DEMO showcased the finest motion works by studios, designers, emerging talent and academies from around the world, for 24 hours on 80 digital screens throughout the station.

DA&TD: Studio Dumbar
CL: Exterion Media NL & Studio Dumbar

① About the glitch: The *Demo* type design is created by a coded way of distortion, which causes intrinsic imperfections.

01
23
45
67
89

DE
MO
Exterion

menu

Bob Mayata (NL)
DBXL (NL)
DIA (US)
Dimitris Papazoglou (GR)
Eike König (DE)
Erich Brechbuhl (CH)
Gilles de Brock (NL)
Gimmewings (ES)
Hansje van Halem (NL)
Hassan Rahim (US)
Hort (DE)
Ines Cox (BE)
Jonathan Castro (PE)
Jordy van den Nieuwendijk (NL)
Jurriaan Hos (NL)
Just van Rossum (NL)
Kenny Brandenberger (CH)
Koos Breen (NL)
Lamm & Kirch (DE)
Lennarts & de Bruijn (NL)
Machine (NL)
Marina Willer (UK)

Random Studio (NL)
Rejane dal Bello (BR)
Roosje Klap (NL)
Sascha Lobe (DE)
Silo (NL)
Spassky Fischer (FR)
Spin (UK)
Staat (NL)
Steffen Hotel (DE)
Strange Attractors (US, NL)
Studio Dumbar (NL)
Studio Feixen (CH)
Studio Harris Blondman (NL)
Studio Moniker (NL)
Sucuk und Bratwurst (DE)
Superlarge (NL)
The Rodina (NL)
Thomas Traum (UK)
Thonik (NL)
Tim Lindacher (DE)
Timo Lenzen (DE)
Toko (AU/NL)

The identity is built around a variable typeface, the shape of which changes according to a self–developed script. Any word entered into the script has its own animated character. While it remains legible at all times, the *DEMO* logo can be distorted at will by anyone visiting the website: simply by moving the cursor. Combined with a strong colour palette – orange and dark blue – the identity has genuine graphic impact.

Part 6.
BE SYMBOLIC

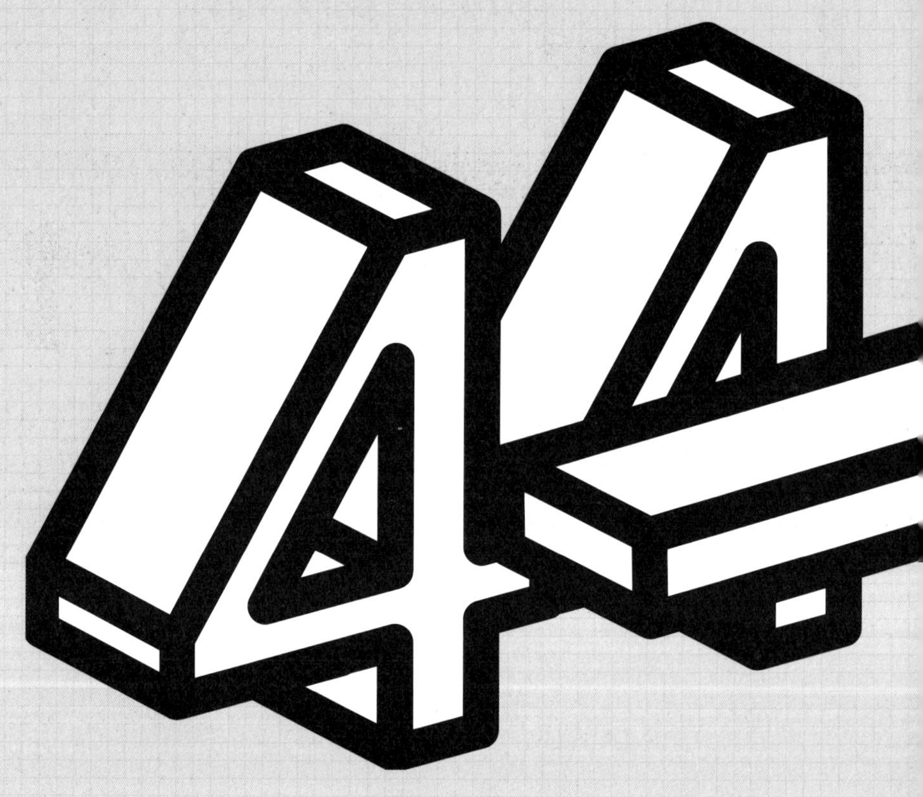

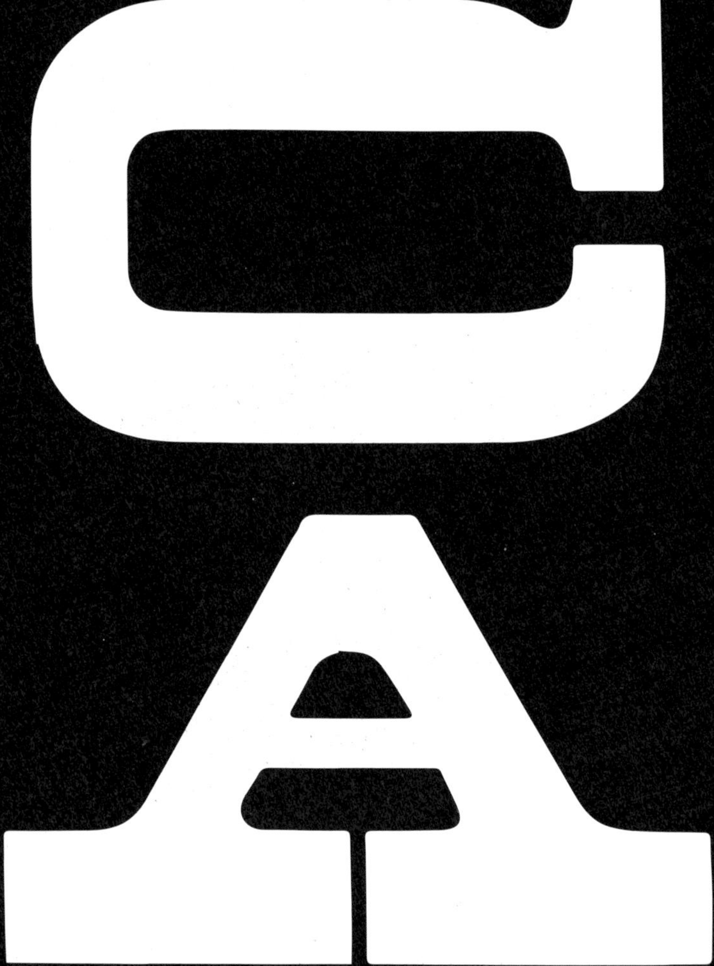
C
A

44. TYPE-FACE

Inspired by the colonialist culture and design elements of Vietnam in the 20th century, the designer creatively applies the most popular and prominent fonts of Ho Chi Minh City before 1975. They select a few letters randomly from the fonts to redesign and use them on the faces of the packaging box. This is why the project is named *Type-face*. It presents a variety of fonts with different historical stories and strikes a balance between the modern and the traditional. In addition, by combining the letters on the box, the consumer would have an interactive experience.

D: Si Tran, Nguyen X- Hoang, Alex Dang
DA: Bratus Agency
CL: Von Viet, Bratus

Bratus
CA-CAO DUY TRÌ
SÁNG-TẠO BỀN LÂU

Bratus

Bratus
Bratus
Bratus

45. ATYPECAL 2020

The designer draws inspiration from modernist design to present a style of combining geometry and typeface. Influenced by the minimalist signage of the Soviet era, the designer explores the relationship between form and style, and designs the characters within non-uniform grids, for the purpose of creating a terse style that can withstand deliberation.

TD: Hermes Mazali

36 Days of Type
Edition 2020

#36daysoftype
#36days_All

@hmazali
Atypecal 20

36 DAYS OF TYPE

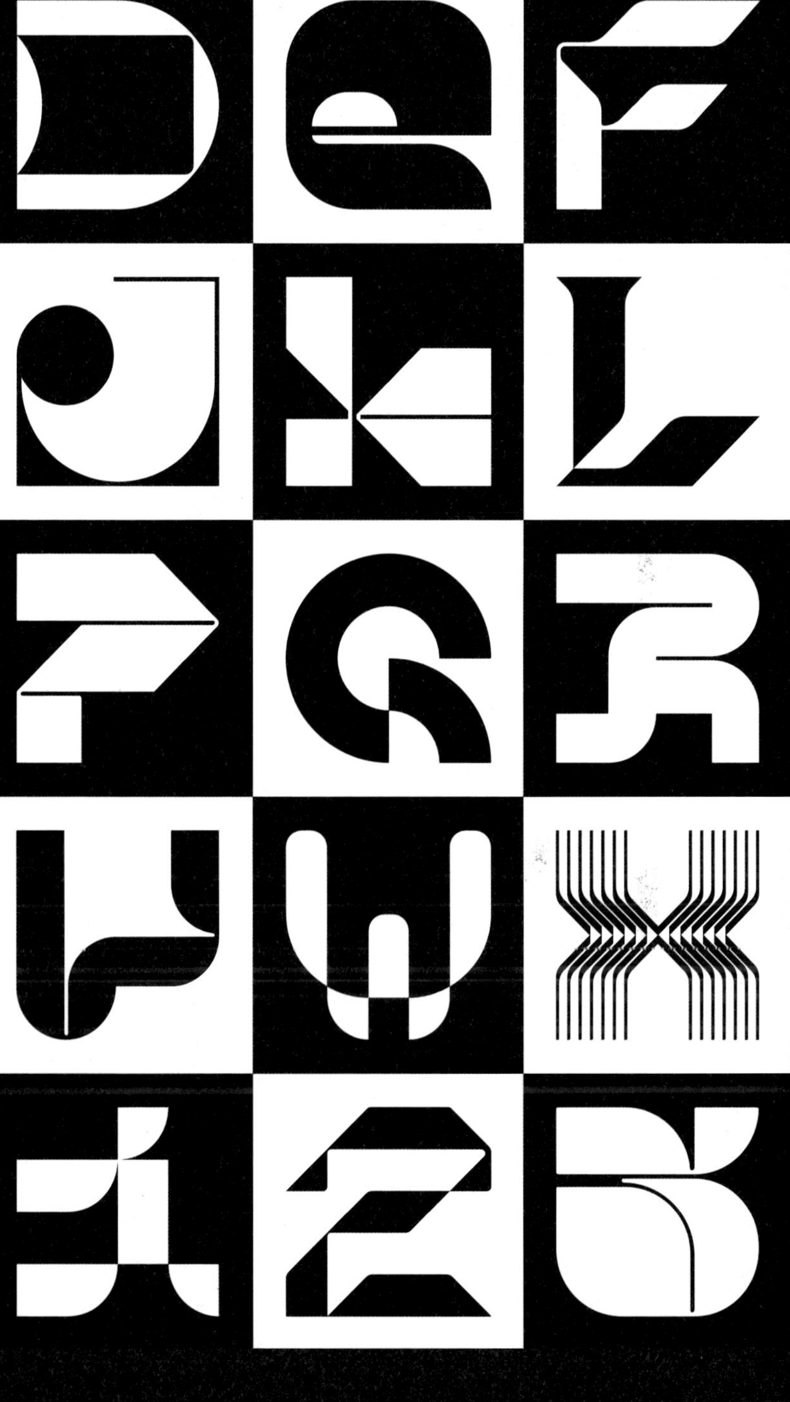

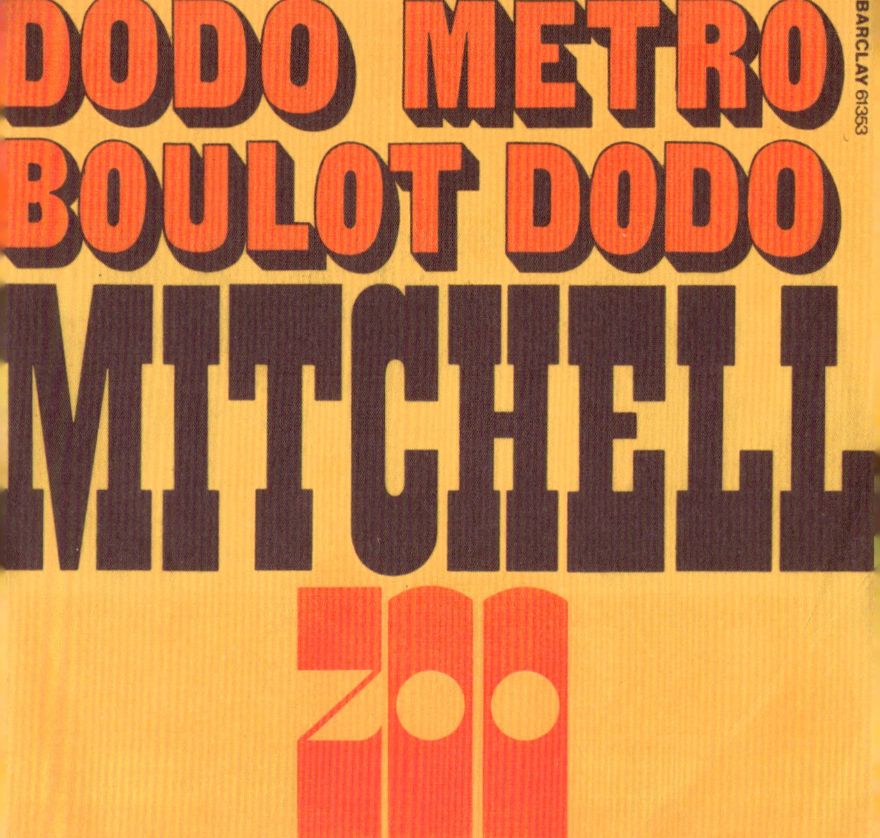
DODO METRO
BOULOT DODO
MITCHELL
ZOO
BARCLAY 61353

46. ZOO

Zoo is a font full of expressive force. The designer starts with the letters "Z" and "O" to set the proportions and characteristics of the entire typeface. The font family includes two varieties of compression and expansion with the highlight of strong contrast between the thick arm and other strokes, giving *Zoo* the moving rhythm.

TD: Quentin Coulombier

121 27

ZOO

HARD TIMES, GOOD TIMES

121.361 L

ZOO

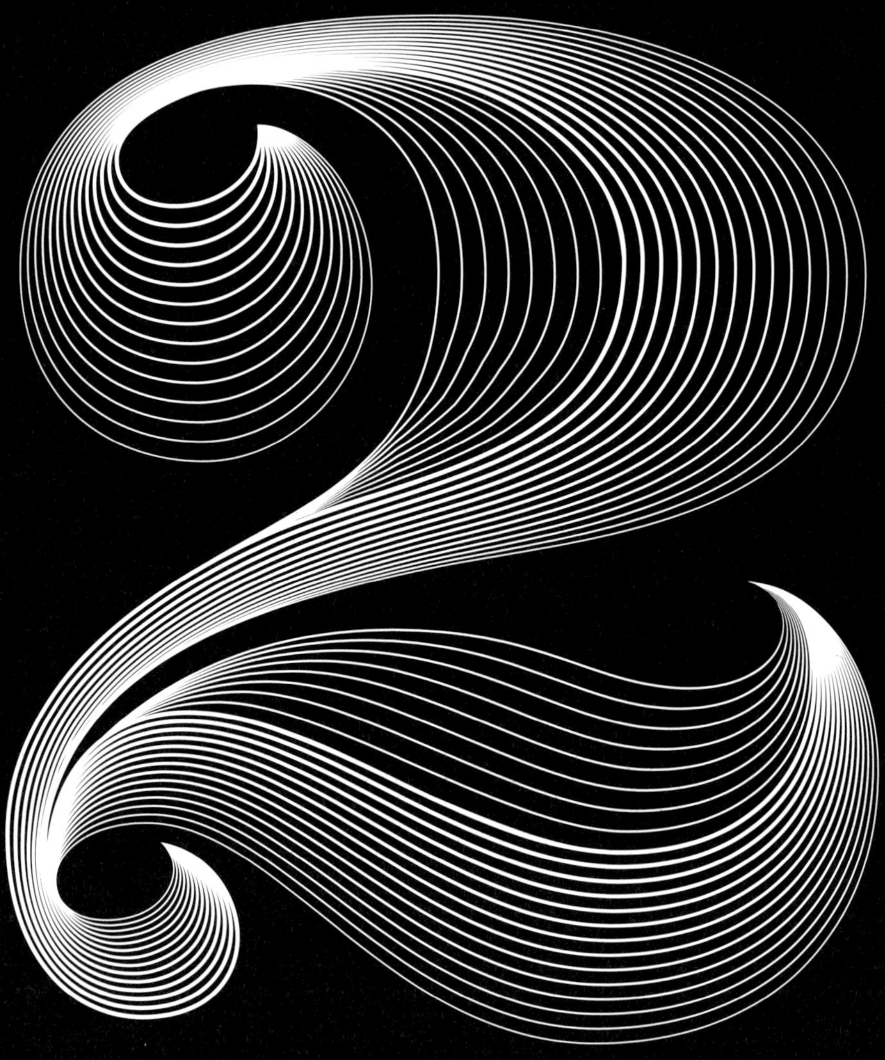

47. NO. 2

As one of the initiators of "TypeThursday" in Bucharest, Romania, the designer is active in type design and outreach education programs. This font is created spontaneously for the "36 Days of Type", highlighting the white space of negative space.

The designer tends to seek inspiration in the urban streets, antique shops, old books, and fonts display. With a preference for the characters of cities and the original aspiration for interest and exploration, she creates a homepage named "Types of Cities", to display the type design with unique aesthetics in the city streetscape.

TD: Bianca Dumitrascu

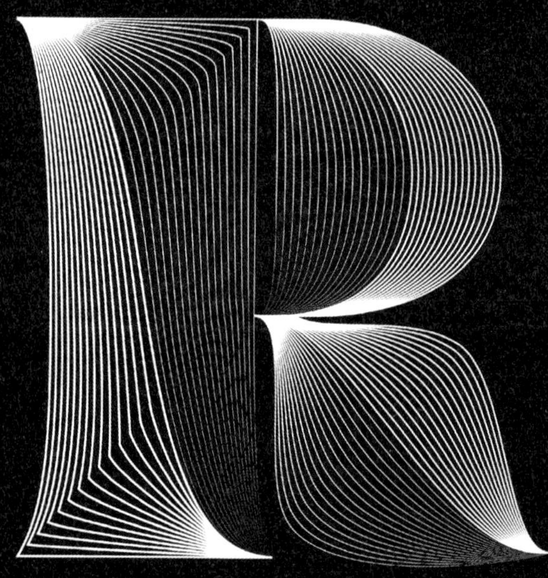

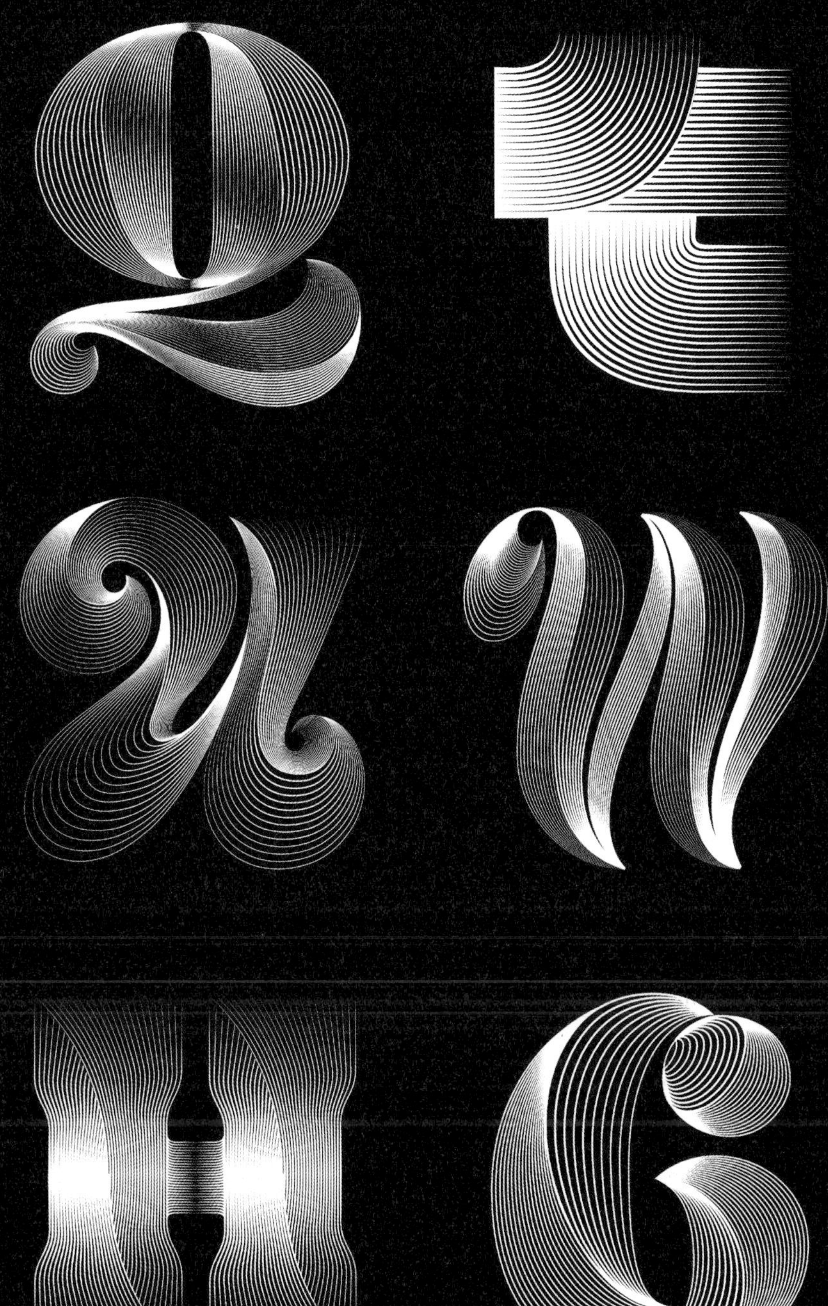

48. BEATRICE DISPLAY

Broke ground in 2018, *Beatrice Display*[1] features internal contrast system that is all at once bold, elegant and refined. It is an exploration of reverse methodologies, combining aspects from canonical calligraphic expansionist systems, inverted contrast, and standard sans-serif grotesks.

The high-contrast Display is reminiscent of the visual oddities of reverse-contrast styles, but explores new territories with its internal contrast system. The stroke emphasis is applied to the outside of the letter-shape, while inside strokes cut through tight spaces with a razor-thin hairline. *Beatrice Display*'s super tight spacing and apertures shine best when used at large sizes.

TD: Lucas Sharp, Connor Davenport
F: Sharp Type Co.

① The designer dedicated the typeface to his mother and named it after her, hoping that her spirit of pursuing beauty and embracing originality will continue.

Rivoluzione!
Lampedusa
Nino Cerruti
Quadrefiore
Piemontèisa
Sant'Antioco
Indipendenti
Conformista

Stylistic Set 1 - Round Dots

i → i Ninjas → Ninjas

Stylistic Set 2 - Alternate Lowercase 'a'

a → a Arazona → Arazona

Stylistic Set 3 - Alternate Uppercase 'W'

W → W Western → Western

The Roman style sets the rules while the italics take these rules in new directions and sometimes break them by emphasizing translation and rotation gestures.

Along with *Beatrice Display*'s release, Beatrice Text was designed as a complementary family with a standard low-contrast cut to function in a wide range of optical sizes. The font family will be further updated and expanded, including the fonts of *Beatrice Headline, Beatrice Deck* as well as its signature italics and new oblique styles.

2018
澳門設計周
EXHIBITION
SEMINAR
LIVE MUSIC
MACAO DESIGN WEEK

Macao Design Week 2018

D: Au Chon Hi
DA: Untitled Macao
CL: Macau Design Week

Cinegiornate Visual Design for Film Festival
D: Paula Del Mas
CL: Cineventi Srl

KELET Visual Design of Documentary
DA: Studio Marina Veziko
CL: Baba Lybeck Productions

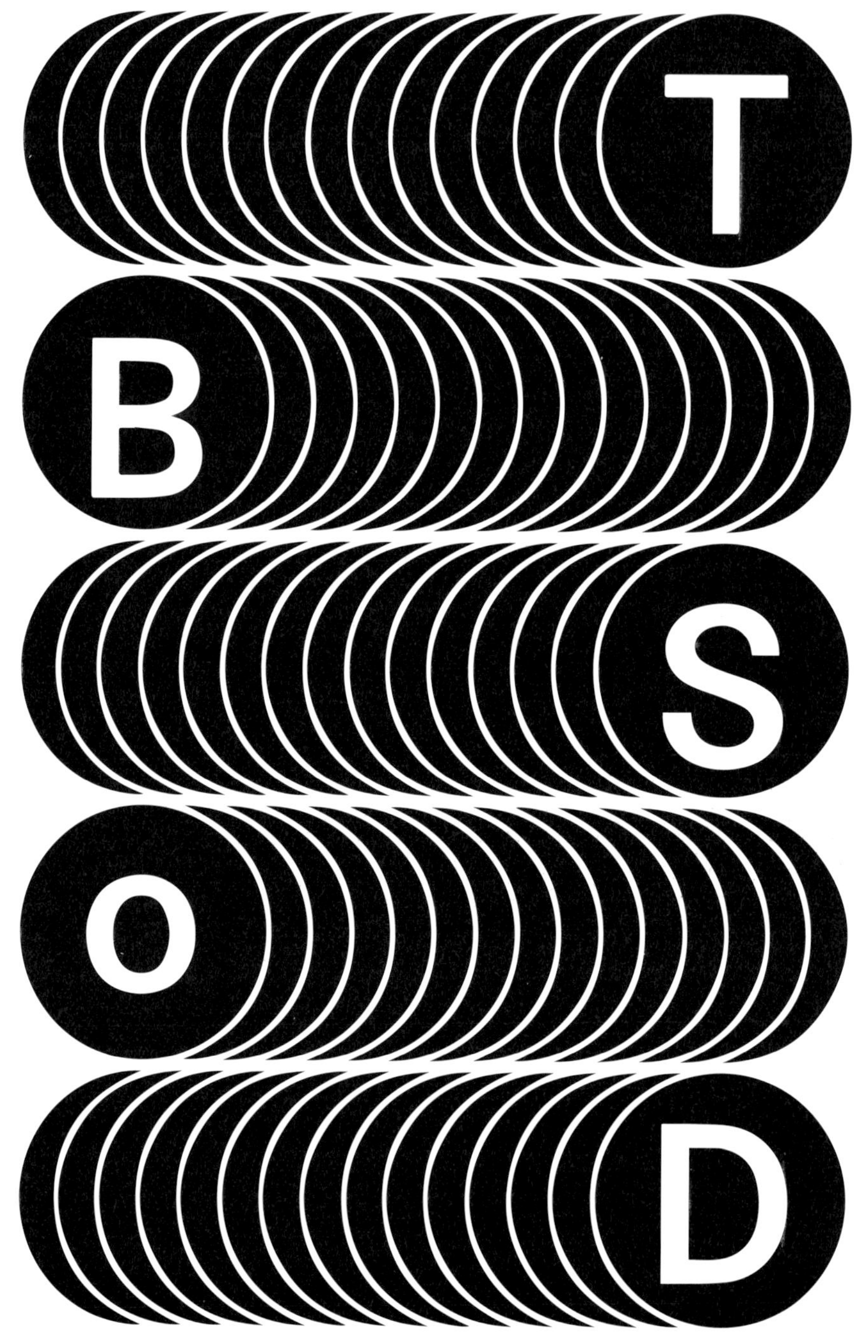
T
B
S
O
D

49. KIOSK

The Basel School of Design

The poster is a promotion design for the Master's program at the Basel School of Design in Switzerland. *Kiosk* used for the main title "The Basel School of Design" was designed by David Gobber. The geometric font is available for retail download. As a font full of expressive force that works well for poster display, *Kiosk* has bold character of its main glyphs is contrasted by thinner parenthesis, hyphens, dashes, arrows, mathematical symbols and other characters.

TD: David Gobber
D: Hoang Nguyen
CL: The Basel School of Design
AD: NGUYENGOBBER

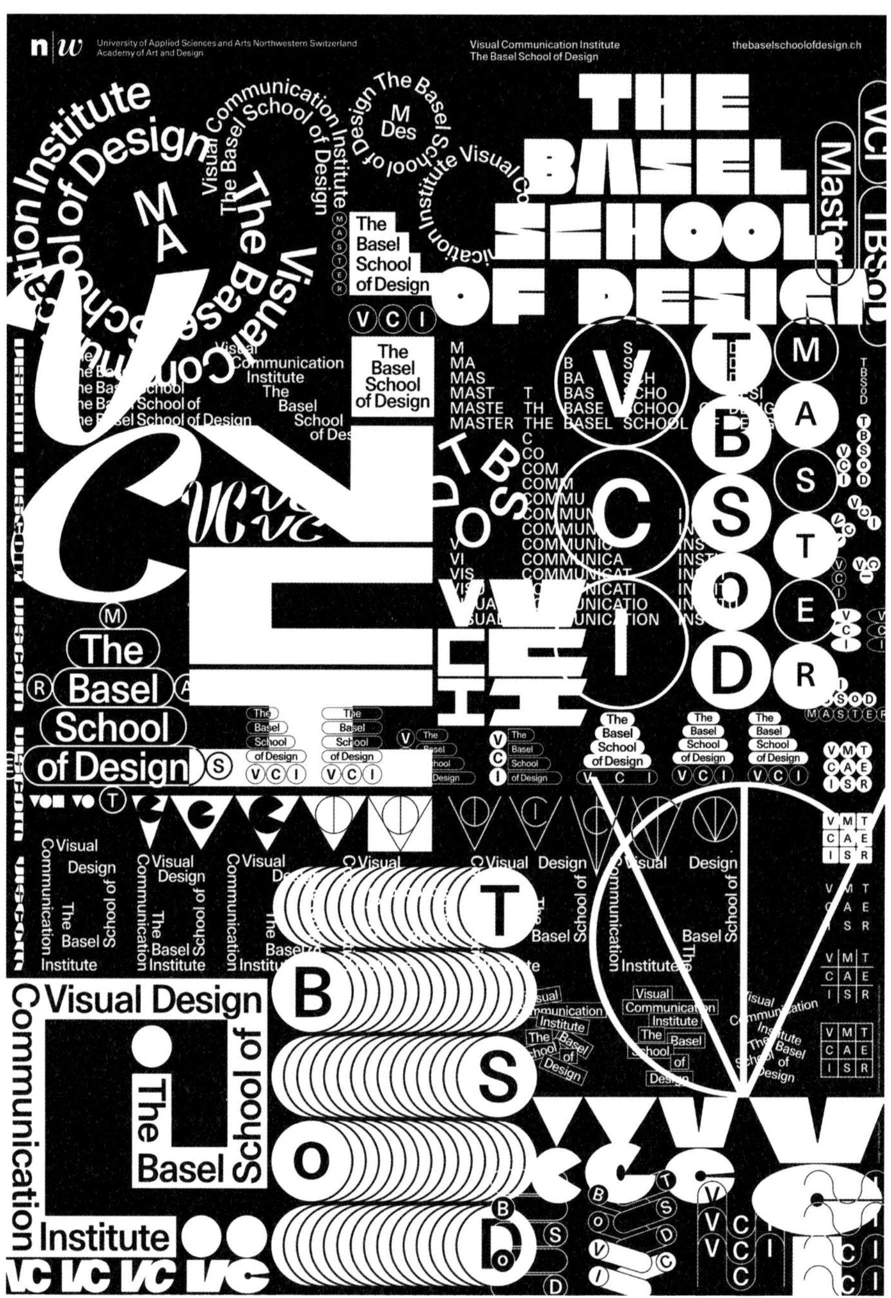
n|w
University of Applied Sciences and Arts Northwestern Switzerland
Academy of Art and Design
Visual Communication Institute
The Basel School of Design
thebaselschoolofdesign.ch
THE BASEL SCHOOL OF DESIGN
The Basel School of Design
VCI
MASTER
Visual Design
Communication
The Basel School of
Institute

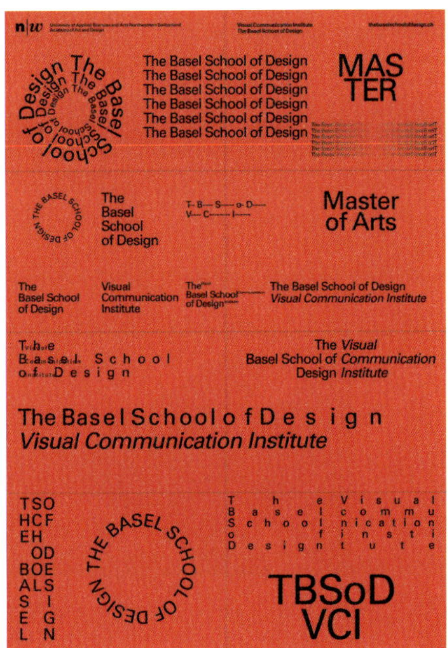

In addition to the main title, some of the logos applies the corporate typeface of the institution *Unica 77* for many variations bespoke letterforms were designed. The type design explores free-floating forms. The calligraphic interpretations of the letters "V" and "C", and the strict geometric structure embodies the unique design spirit of Basel School of Design: pursuing the ideal of openness towards innovative and different design solutions.

50. TOCCO

Tocco is a high contrast variable font available in eight weights. It is the first commercial-used typeface released by the Papanapa Studio. The inspiration comes from the woodblock residues in the workshop. The strokes follow the angles of the wood cut by the machine, where the connections and corners present curved and straight lines with clear angles.

When used as a title typeface or only for display, *Tocco* has angular curves and striking serifs in creating a bold and elegant character. The typeface offers standard ligature and extends multilingual support to basic Latin, Western European languages, and pan-African Latin languages for global accessibility.

DA: Papanapa
CD: Gustavo Garcia
D: Thiago Bellotti

SOLID
WOOD

@ d

Ø ë

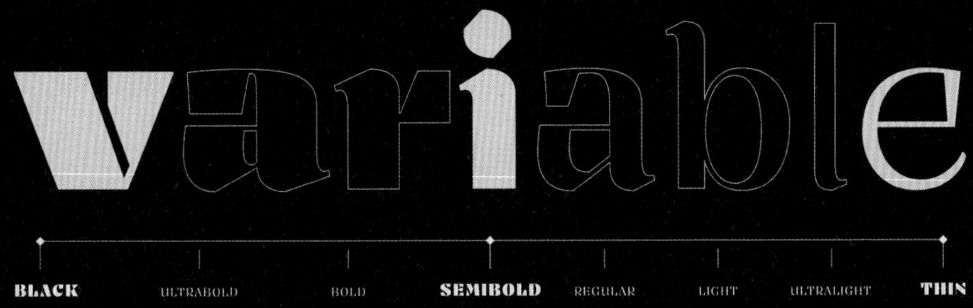

aaaaaaaa
aaaaaaaa
aaaaaaaa
aaaaaaaa

ABCDEFGHIJKLMNOPQRSTUVWXYZ
abcdefghijklmnopqrstuvwxyz
0123456789

,Toc
@

WIP

51. NUMBER 0-10

It is a digital typeface with a square and narrow counter that contrasts strongly with the round and rough outline. The symmetrical beauty of the typeface is based on a rigorous and unique grid system combined with graphics.

TD: Shamil Asgarov

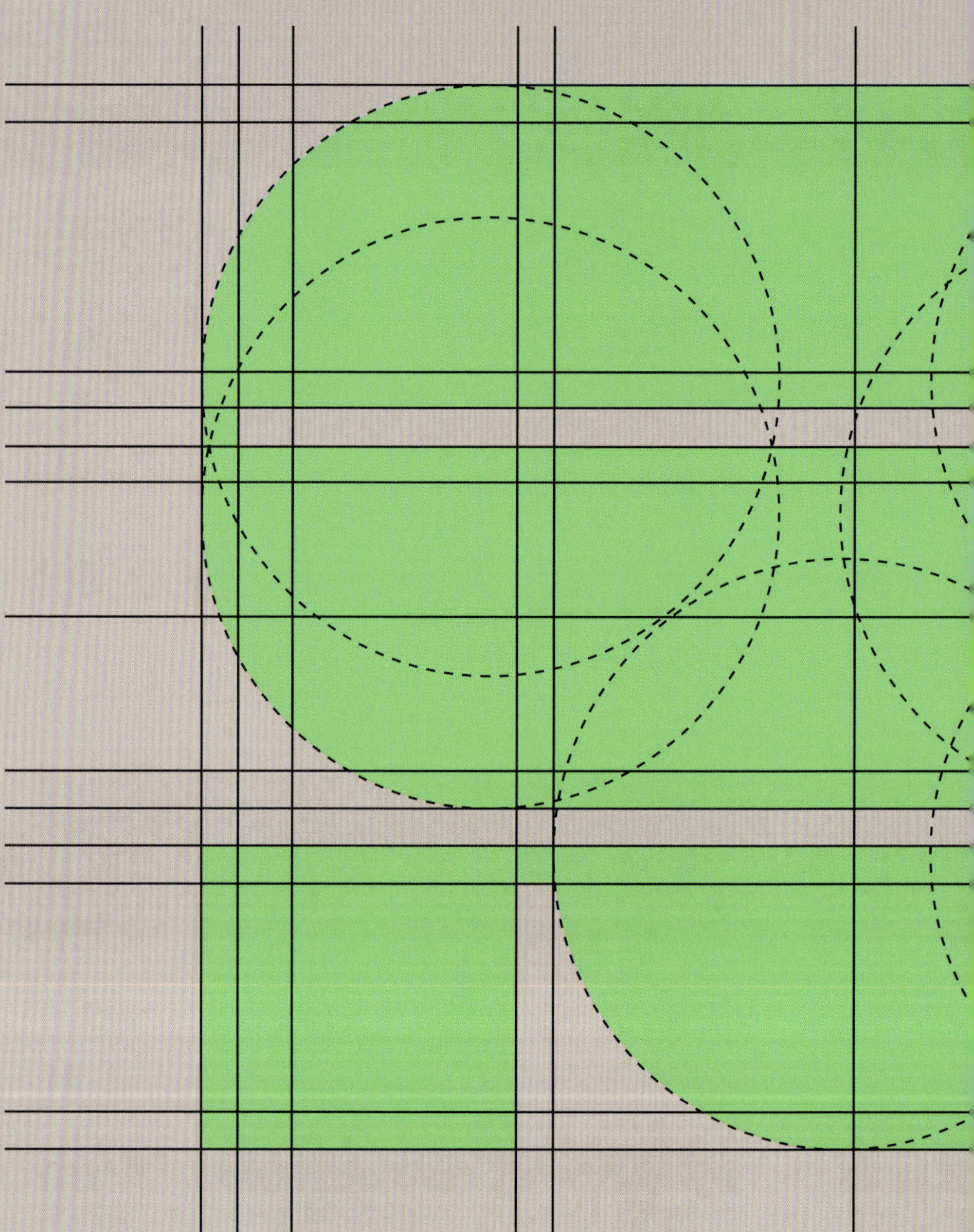

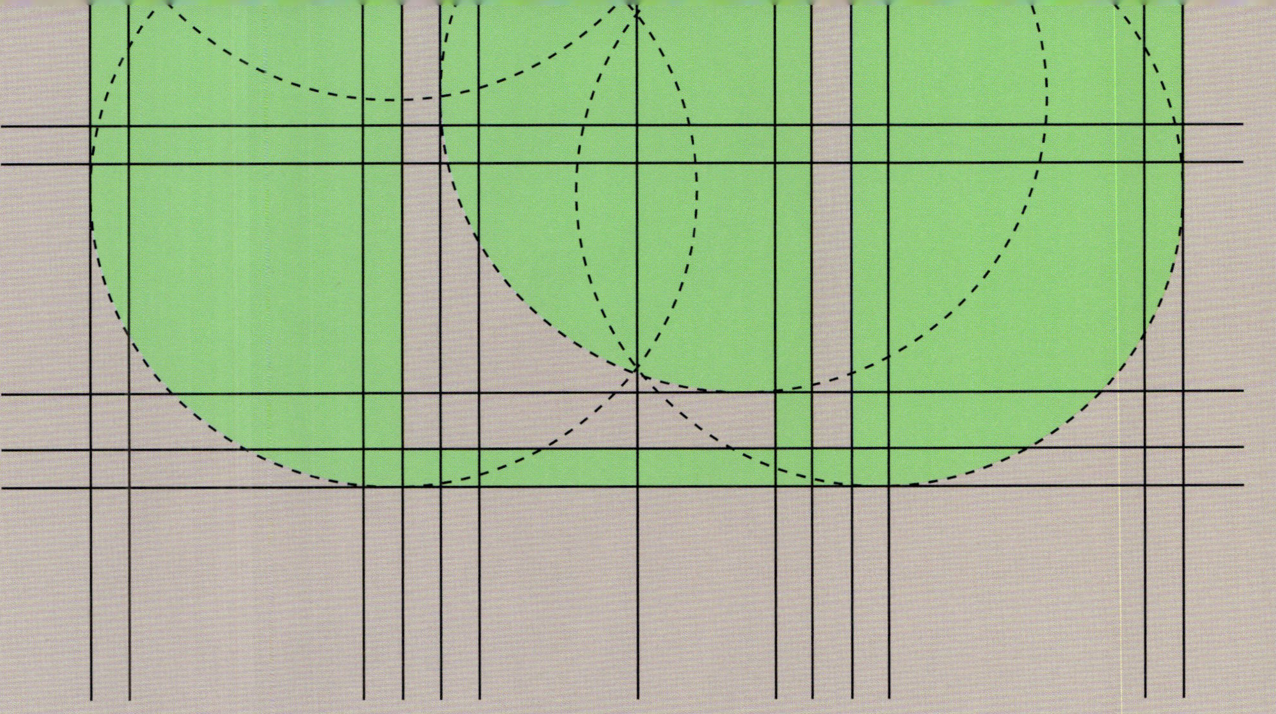

Base grid construction

Number 9

Part 7.
BE RHYTHMIC

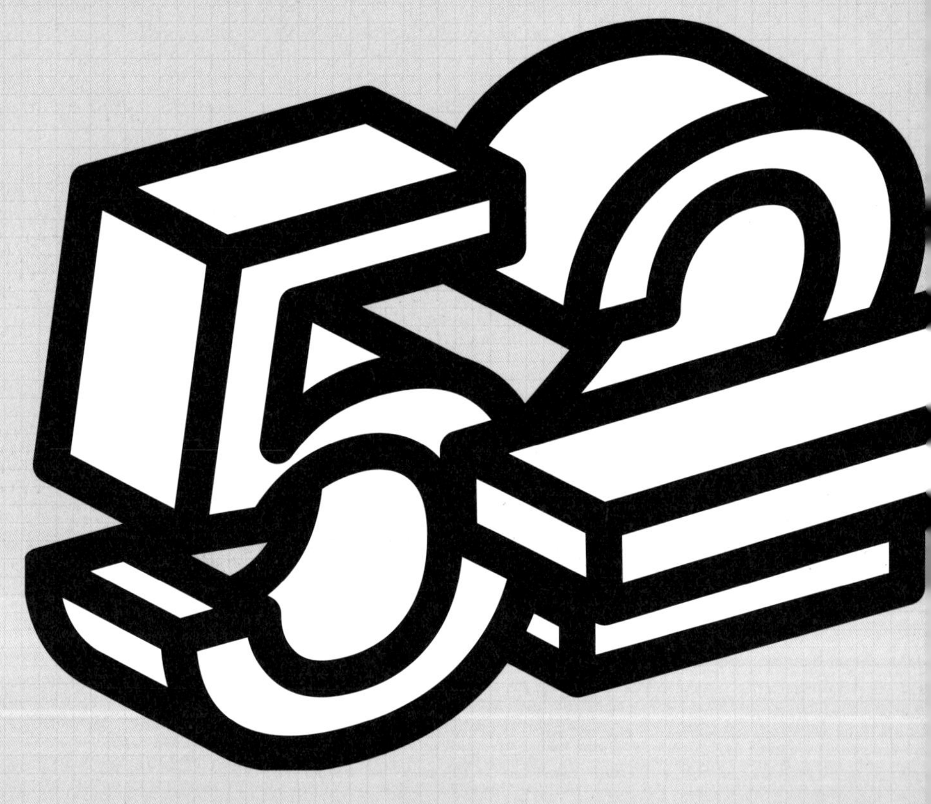

52. COASTLINE

The designer's original plan is to design a help guide for future climate refugees. The plan failed since the required research data were too huge to be dealt with by only one person. The designer unexpectedly found, in a well-sorted global map after the melting of the ice layer, that the coastline of some regions resembled letters. Then the designer attempted to extract three letters, to examine their feasibility and aesthetic direction, and discovered that the glyphs and geographical anecdotes could be combined in such an interesting and organized way. That is how *Coastline* came into being.

TD: Johan Elmehag

A–Z

2°26'17.2"S

16

A

SHORE TO SHORE

AFFECTED COUNTRIES IN THE BAY OF NORTH ITALY INCLUDES ITALY AND SLOVENIA.

17

111°52'06.8"E

Under the Bay of North Italy lies the former Veneto region and by the coastline some rooftops stand out of the water as a reminder of the World Heritage Site of Venice. Recently, it was politically essential to establish cities as close to water as possible. Ironically, the coastal cities are now condemned antiques.

Perhaps the largest cities can be formed into fortified islands, as large walls of water protects the billions of dollar worth of buildings. These types of cities would still be at risk for floods, tsunami and hurricanes. How far can we go to keep our beloved cities? After emptying the city of water after 2, 3 times, can we continue the battle or do we leave the cities for nature to take over and leave for higher altitudes?

BAY OF NORTH ITALY

The coastline type is based on diffe(Z)t coastal regions as they would appear if all th(I)ce in the world melted. The characters a(B)ear in particularly vulnerable areas. The shape is an ex(A)-ggeration, all the ice is not going to melt. (H)owever, it still display areas who will experience a big (C)hange in their coastline in a near future. Each letter carries regional information.

A–Z

0°48'35.5"N

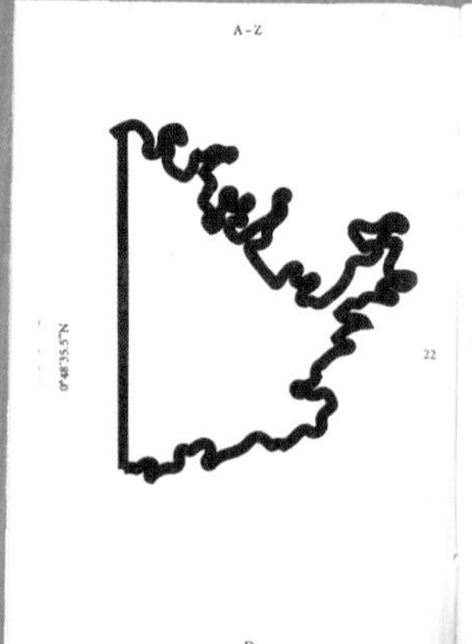

22

D

SHORE TO SHORE

AFFECTED COUNTRIES IN FORMER CENTRAL BORNEO INCLUDES BORNEO.

23

114°35'15.9"E

Changed weather patterns in the Pacific contribute to drought in Indonesia. Sadly, it is also expected that an increased number of tsunamis will occur in Oceania. All life that is below ten meters above sea level is likely to be destroyed. But above 10 meters, are not safe as well when super hurricanes are on the entrance.

When we are still in this part of the world, it is also important to mention the low-lying islands in the Pacific. Tuvalu, Kiribati, Marshall Islands, Tokelau and Maldives are some of the archipelagos that are completely underwater in our new world.

FORMER CENTRAL BORNEO

This is a typeface with the implication of a doomsday warning. The designer preset the background of the melting of the global ice layer and converted the shorelines of the coastal areas that would be severely affected into letters. Although it is seemingly impossible for the ice layer to disappear due to melting, these areas will be hit hard when disaster strikes. Behind each letter is a profile of a real area, and the fonts are outlined based on the National Geographic and the information visualized from the map website, floodmap.net.

Although the type design would be finalized with compromise and abandonment, it retains the basic functions and images. It is kind of similar to the reason that society must make changes to maintain the operation.

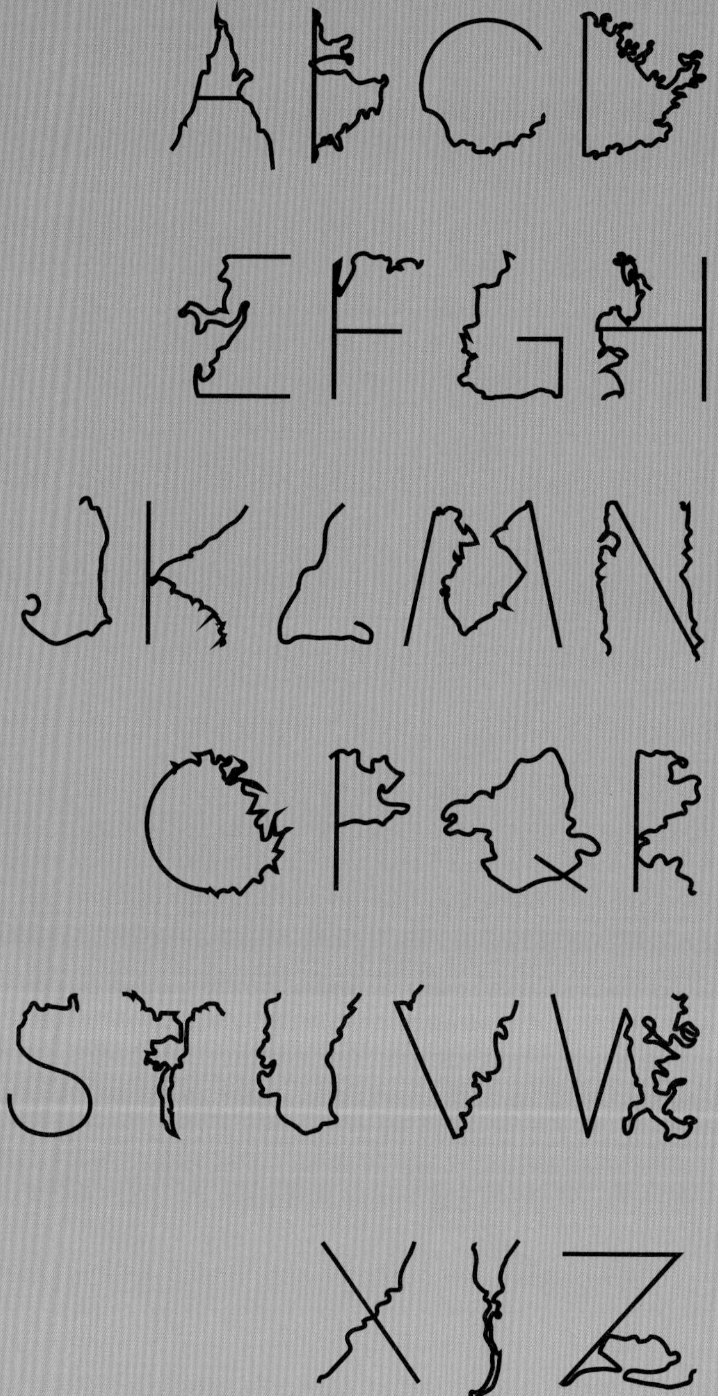

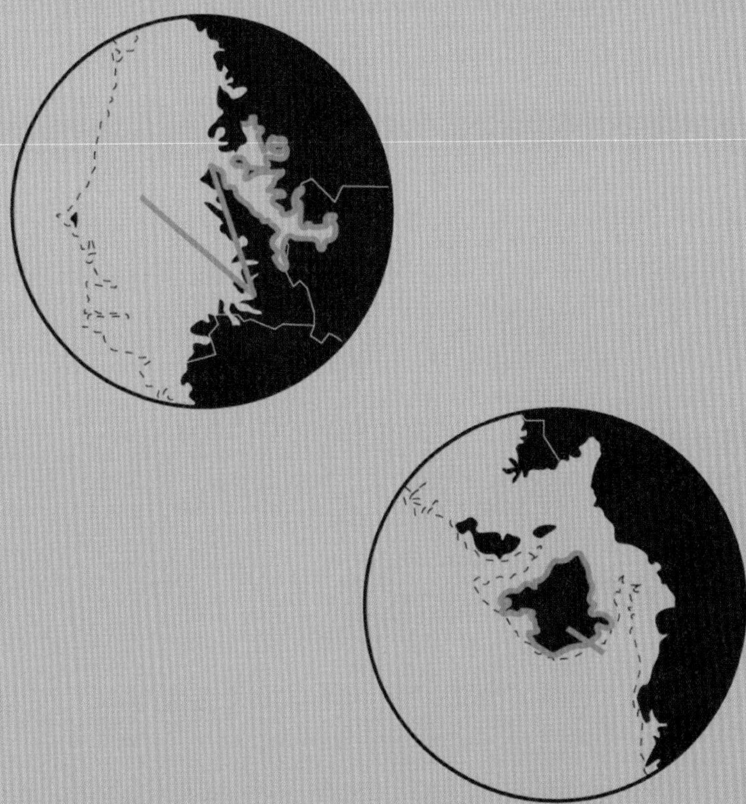

Coastline was designed with three letters. The designer set a few rules, such as determining that the coastline of the type line should be selected worldwide; and establishing a measurable word spacing and an aesthetically pleasing letter format.

The designer created four fonts and experimented with serif but decided on a simpler line to avoid distracting the core message with the addition of other elements.

To the person
in the bell jar,
blank and stopped
as a dead baby,
the world itself
is a bad dream.

53. ESTHER

BOOK DESIGN OF *THE BELL JAR*

Based on the font *Lora*, the designer created *Esther*, a font with a sense of liquidity. After a number of experimental deformation, the font was designed to echo the stories of characters in the book suffering from mental illness, resulting in unreadable graphic text that symbolized the plot.

TD&D: Aniko Mezo

I began to think vodka
was my drink at last. It
didn't taste like anything,
but it went straight down
into my stomach like
a sword swallowers'
sword and made me feel
powerful and godlike.

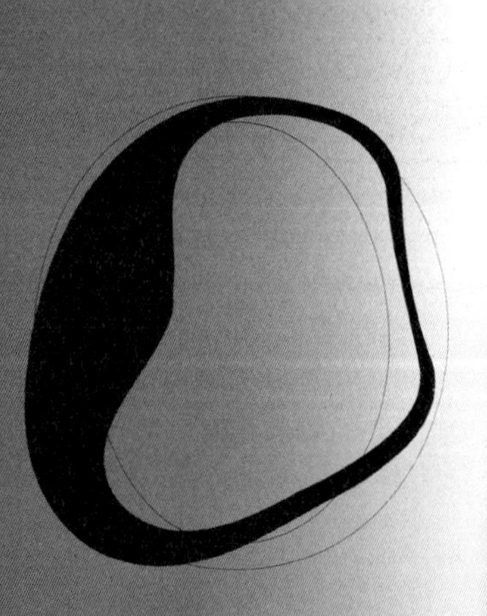
Oo

by Sylvia Plath

In addition to being used in the cover design of novels, the font has the details and process of design printed separately. The two books are placed in a transparent plexiglass box, and the twisted letters on the covers imply the perspective of the protagonist through the mirror reflection of the glass, which in visual form echoes the title of *The Bell Jar* and the theme of psychological distortion of the characters.

54. PRINTEMPS

The design was inspired by the love of the typefaces in the Art Nouveau[①] period. Fascinated by the flowing, overlapping lines of the era, the designer created the serif font, redefining the classic in a modern style.

The basic structure follows the humanistic rules of type design, and the experimental details make the font more recognizable. A large number of ligatures and matching glyphs reflect the profound Art Nouveau style.

TD: Julian Stiber

① Art Nouveau, prevalent in the late 19th and early 20th century, is characterized by its dynamic, wave-like, flowing lines. It has been named one of the most innovative forerunners of the cultural movements in the 20th century, along with Expressionism, Cubism, and Surrealism.

Ligatures

AMULETTE

vermeil Dijon

rejeté figuier

avenue charisme

marrons siffler

Base Glyphs

A B C D E F G 0 1 2 3 4 5 6 7

H I J K L M N 8 9 ! ? „ " § $ %

O P Q R S T U & ( ) [ ] / \ | + - ,

V W X Y Z . : ; # * < > ≤ ≥ « »

a b c d e f g h i € £ ↑ → ↓ ← ↔ ↕

j k l m n o p q r @ ¶ © ™ ® † ‡ ∞

s t u v w x y z

LOVE-SONGS

NICHT NICHT

A1	PROXY I	5:49
2	SELBSTAUFLÖSER TEIL 2	6:25
3	DAS LABYRINTH	4:46
4	NICHT NICHT	3:11
B1	TISCH MIT DREI BEINEN	4:08
2	PROXY II	8:28
3	OG	8:14

All tracks composed, arranged, played, produced and recorded by Love-Songs.

Berkshire
Kent
Middlesex
Norfolk
Rutland
Suffolk
Yorkshire

55. VOYAGE

Voyage was released in 2019, featuring curved lines full of romance, like an attractive journey on the road trip. As a display font, it can be used in large sizes, especially for heading or short text. The designer created 55 unique ligatures and 26 variants, as well as the lowercase "e" and curling "h" with fine, thin strokes and maximum contrast from an adventurous perspective. As an OpenType, it allows users to choose and adjust the glyphs as required.

TD: Jeremy Schneider
F: VJ Type

Sud ?

Ouest !

Ponctuations

Nord.

y style 2

Molfetta

M alternates

a alternates

Originally inspired by the creative research for client projects, *Voyage* has a lot of elaborate details included. The curvilinear typeface conveys the sensory impression of travel: the surge of the ocean and the moment when the waves rise and fall. It is a combination of rich details, alluring curves, swirling glyphs, and dancing flames.

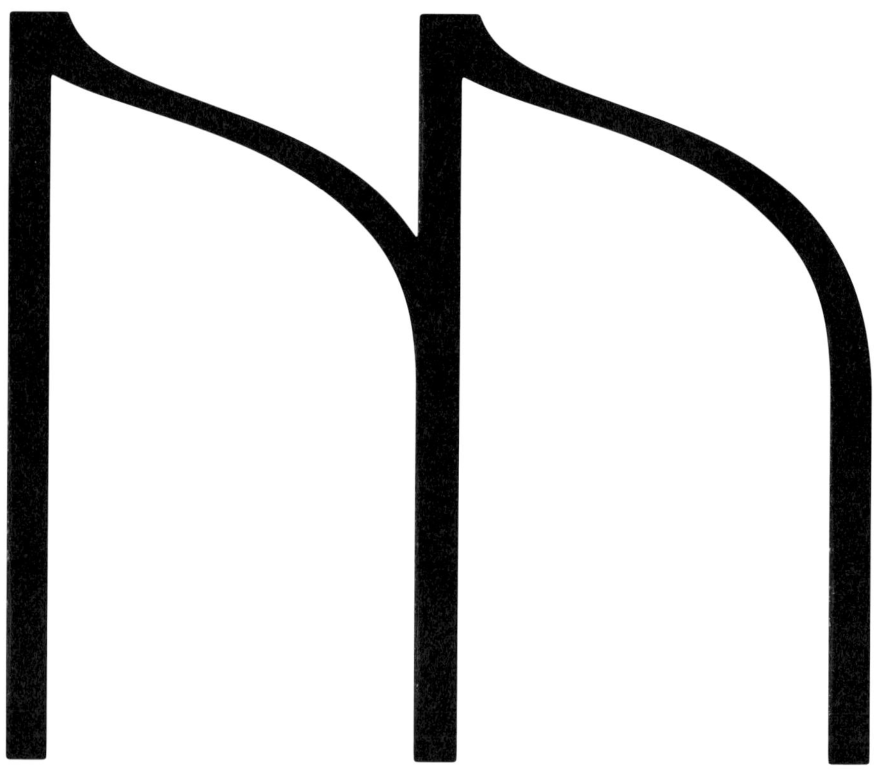

56. DYADE

Dyade literally means the close bond between people, like that between parents and child. As for its extended meaning, the font combines curvy and avant-garde futuristic elements and shows the intersection of different art domains. The modern and elegant brushwork is perfect for heading.

TD: Stefanie Vogl

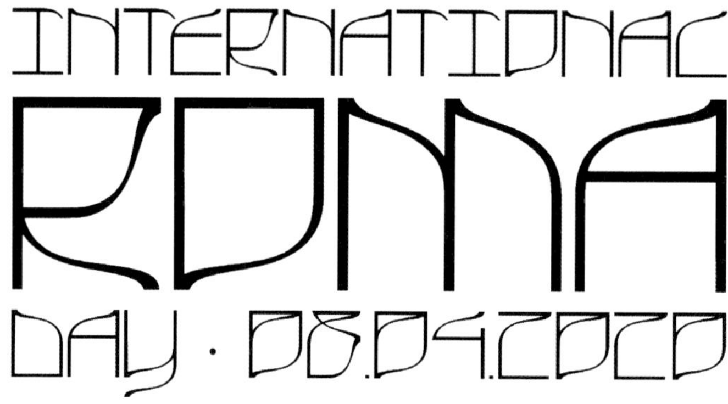

EVEN TODAY THERE IS STILL DISCRIMINATION AND VIOLENCE AGAINST ROMANI PEOPLE IN EUROPE. LET'S STOP THE HATE AND TREAT EVERY PERSON WITH KINDNESS AND RESPECT NO MATTER WHAT SKIN COLOR OR CULTURE THEY HAVE. THE FIRST MEETING OF ROMANI PEOPLE WAS HELD 30 YEARS AGO IN ENGLAND

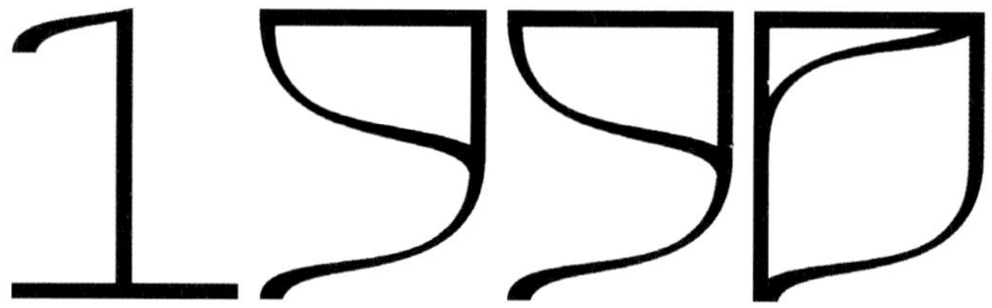

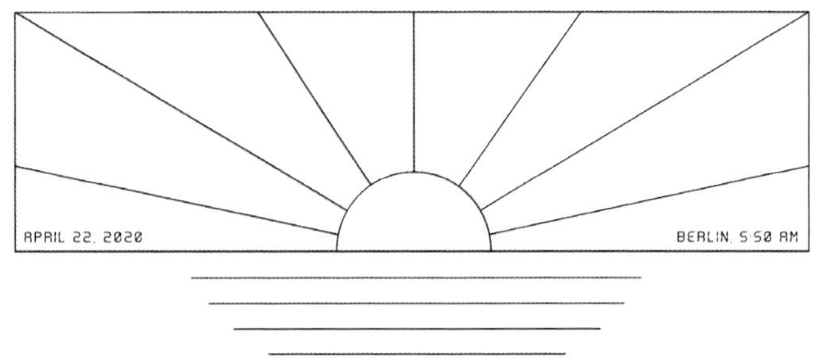
APRIL 22, 2020
BERLIN, 5:50 AM

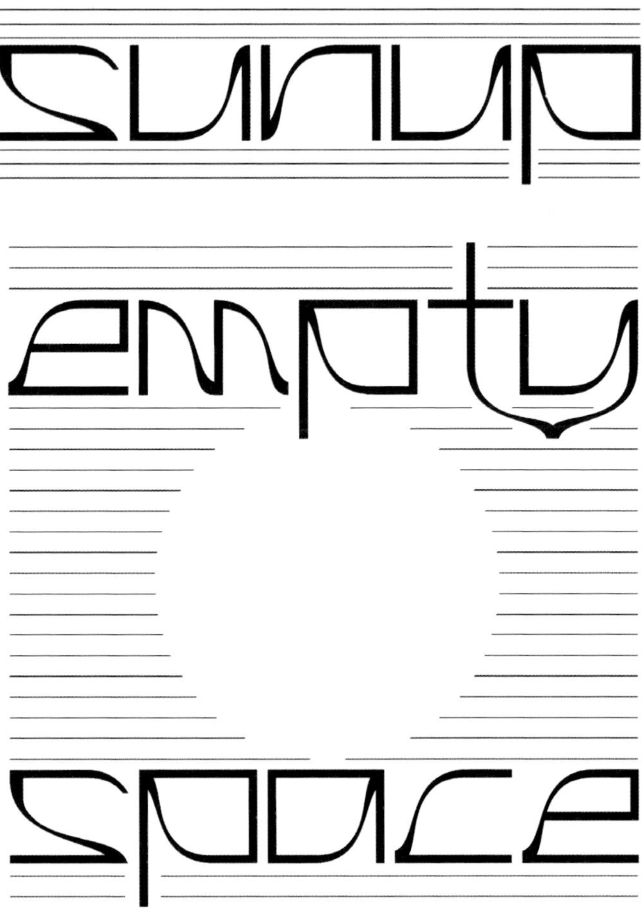
sunup
empty
space

57. ALEKJA SERIF

The font is inspired by the resumes that design companies receive every day. They screen the talent just like the fonts that are installed in a computer, while designers want to be the best candidate for a project just like the fonts.

Enlightened by tarot cards and astrology, the designer uses soft and light glyphs to create a font full of flexibility, elegance, and mystery.

TD: Alexia Lullo

abc
ghijk
opq
vw

def

lmn

rstu

xyz

ti th ct ve

&! ae oe

1234567890

#€€€€€

I AM PERFECT & FOR BIG TITLES

also for the smallest one.

GRAND SLANG

the typeface SPECIMEN

c/o nikolas typefaces www.nikolastype.com

58. GRAND SLANG

Grand Slang is a new typeface that boldly discovers, and reshapes the essence of the mid-20th century American calligraphy. It inherits the beauty and warmth of contemporary designers Oscar Ogg and William A. Dwiggins, by integrating the grotesque and serifs in over 310 characters, including non-graphic combinations of upper and lower-case letters, ligatures, numbers, and symbols.

TD: Nikolas Wrobel
F: Nikolas Type

CONSCIOUS
App oach.
Use orm
fo ere
En ent.
NO NO
CONSCIOUS
Approach.
GRAND
Slang
N°4
FLEUR
d'Oranger

A FLOWER DOES NOT
THINK OF COMPETING TO
THE FLO... EXT TO IT,
IT J... OMS.

A FLO... ES NOT
THINK OF ... PETING TO
THE FLOWER NEXT TO IT,
IT JUST BLOOMS.

① Discrete ligatures are rounding up the appearance.

② *Grand Slang* comes with lots of playful options for typographic expression like the displayed alternative for the "T".

APOSTLE
DIGITAL
Tim Nagle
Executive Producer / Founder
M +61 422 722 100
E tim@apostledigital.com
W apstl.co

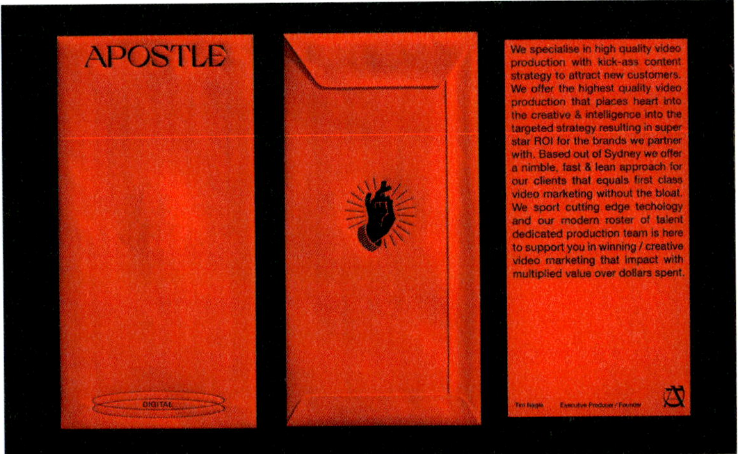

Grand Slang is used in a brand design created by Mubien Studio for Apostle Digital, a Sydney-based film production studio. The studio's name is in *Grand Slang* with *Neue Helvetica* and is printed in Gmund's Electric Blood Paper, with the crafts of punching and gilding.

Apostle Digital Studio Brand Visual Design
DA: Mubien Studio
CL: Apostle Digital

fog

59. FOGTYPE

Fogtype is a modular typeface. The basic format skillfully breaks the rules. The constant repetition from letters to graphics creates a continuous rhythmic beauty, and the end is full of artistic sense.

TD: Jimbo Bernaus

ABC
DEFG
HIJKLM
NOPQRS
TUVW
XYZ

FOGTYPE

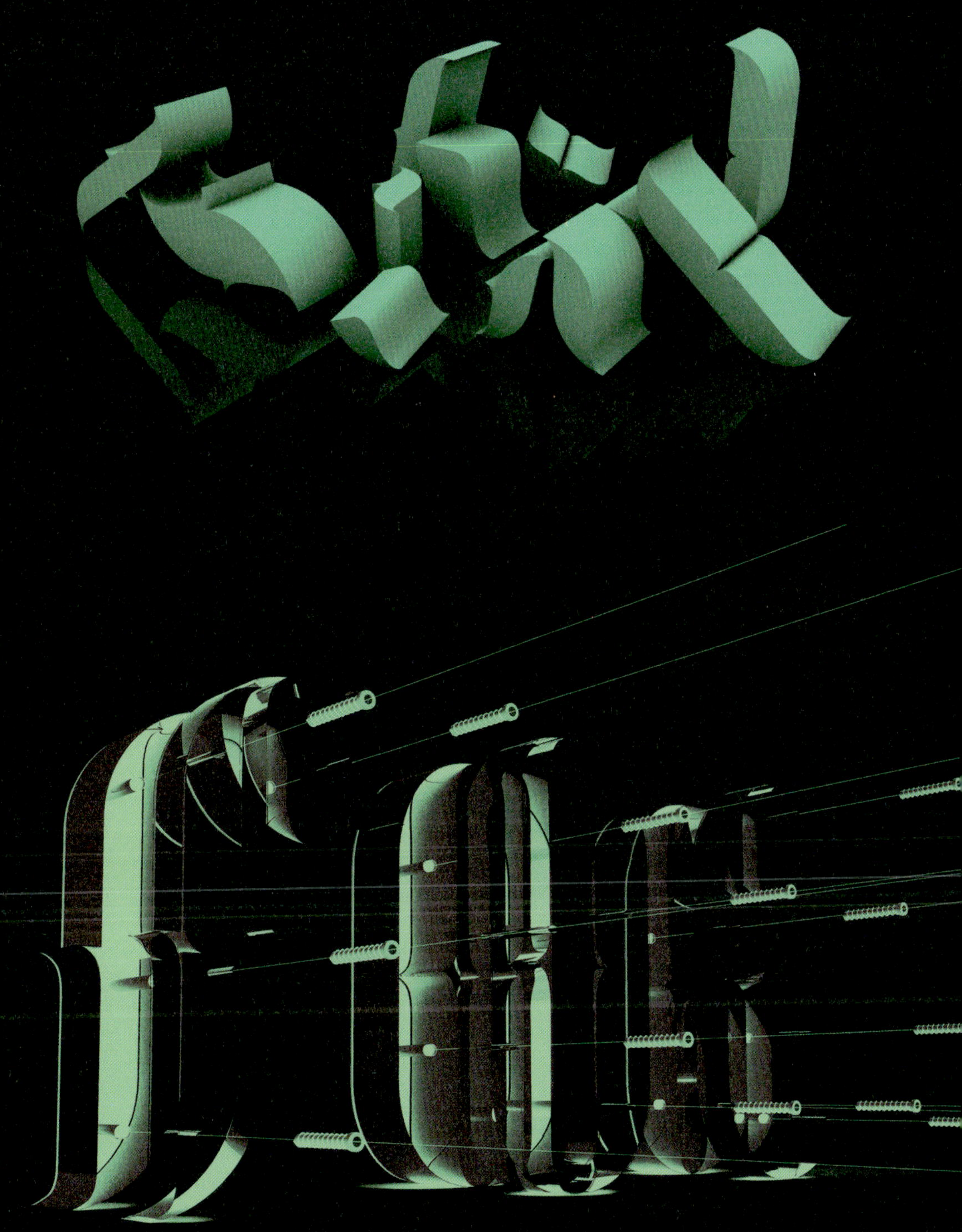

60. RESPIRA BLACK

The design of *Respira Black* was inspired by a mix of calligraphic models, with the uppercase resembling the handwritten *Uncial*, and the lowercase drawing on a distinctive Spanish blackletter which is often found in illuminated manuscripts of Andalusia.

TD: Lucas Sharp, Wei Huang
F: Sharp Type Co.

Respira Black

Take Action

Adopt energy-saving habits. Make it a habit to turn off the lights.

Walk or bike whenever possible. You reduce your carbon footprint, and your improve your health.

Insulate yourself and your home. By properly insulating your home, you ensure that heat stays in or out depending on the season. Do this by purchasing windows coverings that will block out or keep in warmth, and by sealing any existing cracks.

Stylistic Set 01 - Alternate Lowercase 'a' and 'k'

a → a Alabama → Alabama

k → k Kentucky → Kentucky

Stylistic Set 02 - Alternate Lowercase 'g'

g → g Oregon → Oregon

Stylistic Set 03 - Alternate Uppercase 'N'

N → N Nevada → Nevada

Stylistic Set 04 - Alternate Uppercase G

G → G Granada → Granada

Designer Lucas Sharp first came across this unique style of typeface in Granada Cathedral, Spain. Blackletter was originally used for text settings, and its modern use is almost exclusively for display. As a result, the existing text models are more decorative than the originals. The manuscript the designers found are strikingly beautiful and skillful, with foundational storkes simple and plain.

Respira Black takes after this no-frills, no-noise, yet confident approach. Its design also exudes a certain warmth and ephemerality in the movement of the strokes. The letters, which appear to be stenciled actually reference the style of razor-sharp hairlines has gradually fade into sight.

As the
west
burns
September 11th, 2015

Just Because

The World

Runs On

Oil Doesn't

Mean Oilmen

Should Run

The World

"Peri's [illegible] Oil"
-The [illegible] / Busdriver

Respira Black
Specimen

Designed by
Erik Carter

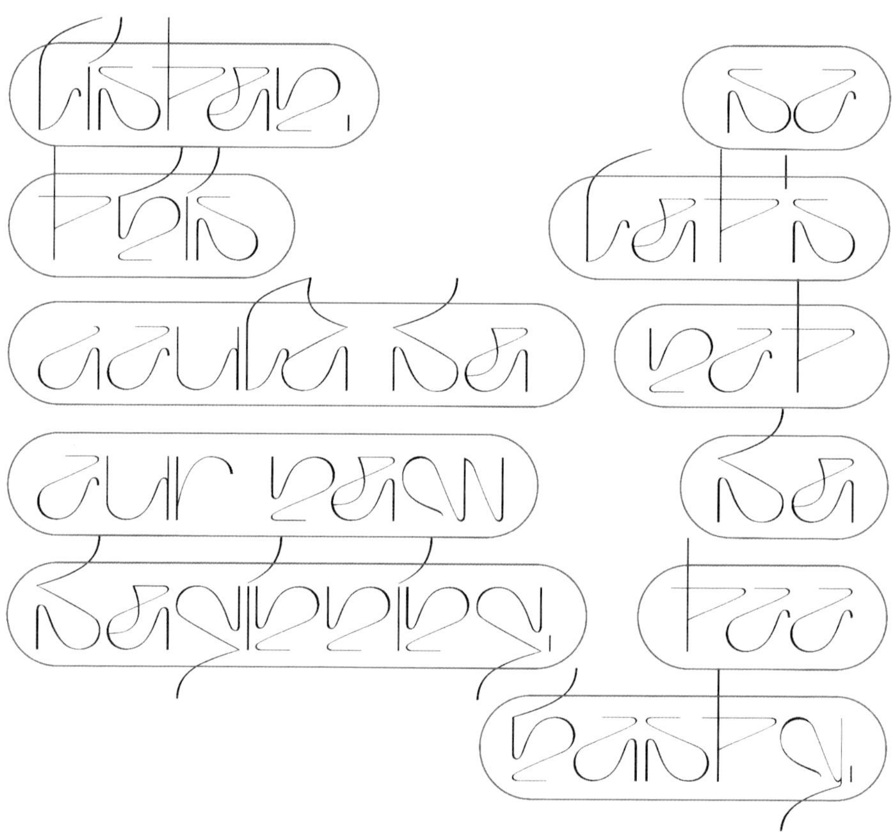

61. AUTARK

The word "Autark" means the emotion to be self-sufficiency in German. In the experimental design process, the designer draws different shapes on a piece of paper and then selects the font that best displays emotion. *Autark* is a powerful typeface that can be displayed alone. It can also be used in combination with such typefaces as sans serif, especially fits for huge headine and titling that demand an aura of craftsmanship.

TD: Stefanie Vogl
DA: OMFD Official

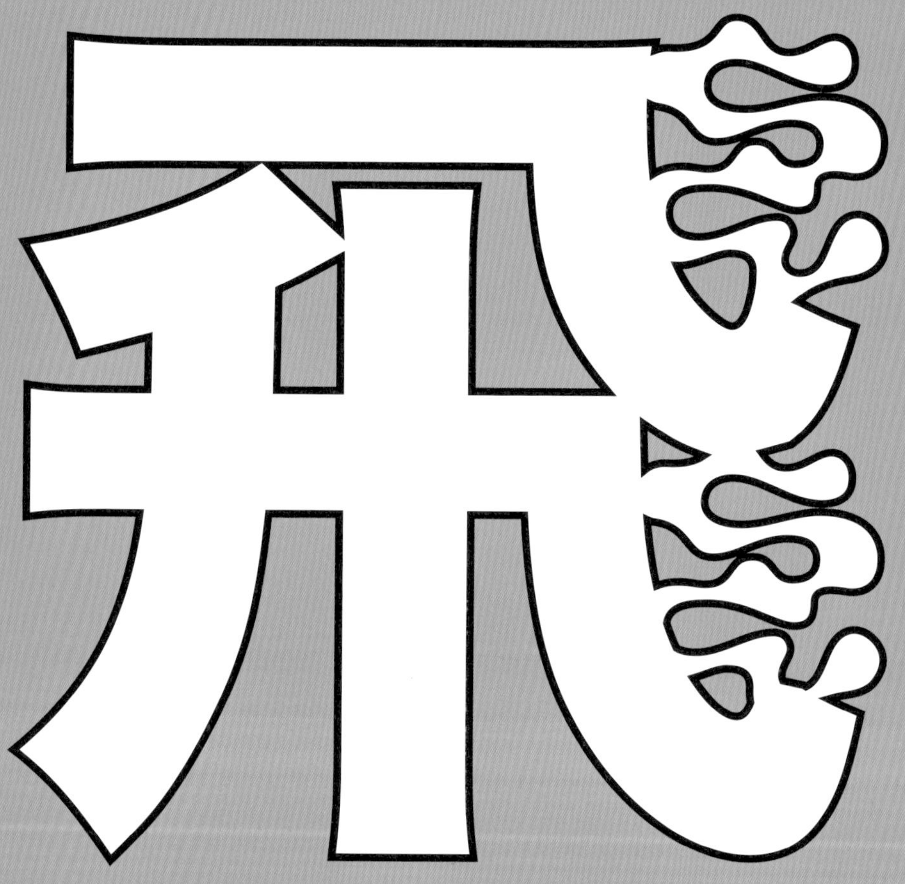

62. LYNO

Sunset Rollercoaster

Sunset Rollercoaster is a band from Taiwan, China, and the designer is dedicated to creating a rollercoaster feel through the poster for a tour in South Korea, which echoes the band's name and style.

D: Dokho Shin

SUNSETROLLERCOASTER
落日飛車
HELICOPTER RECORDS
LIVE IN KOREA 2018
2018년 6월 10일(일) 7pm, KT&G 상상마당 라이브홀 입장료: 예매 44,000원 현매 55,000원

LIEDBASEL
www.liedbasel.ch | Motto 2019: Die Gedanken sind frei | info@liedbasel.ch
LIEDBASEL
Internationales Festival
23. Mai – 26.
Acker
Hotel
Sulger-Stiftung
Nicati - de Luze
LIEDBasel ist eine zeitgemässe und interdisziplinäre Auseinandersetzung mit der Kunstform Lied.
LIEDBasel: LIEDSalon, LIEDRezital, LIEDAcademy, LIEDOnDemand, LIEDLabor

Part 8.
BE EXPRESSIVE

63. EPHEMERA DISPLAY

The style of *Ephemera Display* is inspired by centuries of typographic tradition. Its letterfomrs evoke the characterisitc of blackletter Gothic from mediaval, while also incorporating features of humanist serif type from the Renaissance. It is a unique blend of the retro and modern.

When designing new fonts, designers tend to look back on the previous works for inspiration and guidance. This process enables designers to better understand the historical basis of fonts, which is of great help to spur new ideas.

TD: Barrett Reid-Maroney

abcdefhgij
klmnopqrs
tuvwxyz
123456789

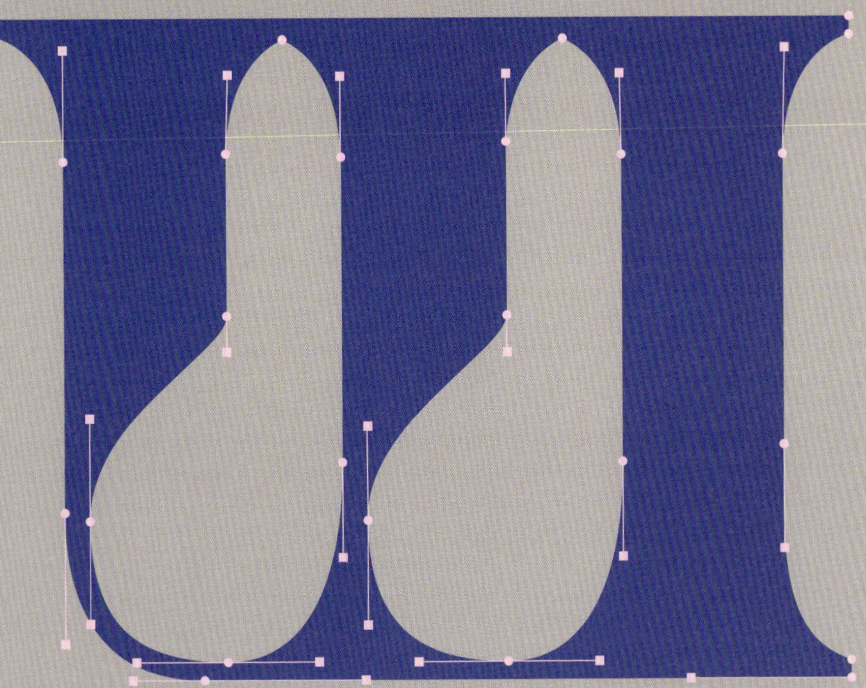

The designer focuses on the visual consistency of each letterform, including the negative space between letters matching the space within in counters of the letterfomrs themselves. The designer hopes the fonts to achieve the best visual balance while visually Interesting and dynamic.

fa fe

ff ca

fo fu

ra tte

fr at

ba fi

abcdefghijklmnopqrstuvwxyz

abcdefghijklmnopqrstuvwxyz

0123456789.,:;!?'"''"" @_&#

%*+-×÷=~<>/\(){}[]$¢€£¥©®™

àáâãäåæçèéêëìíîïñòóôõöøœùú

ûüýÿþđłšž¡¿«»‹›¤•°±–¶§‰/——

àáâãäåæçèéêëìíîïñòóôõöøœùú

ûüýÿþđłšžß|^ˆˇ¨˜`´¸˛,„…|†‡

64. LANGULAIRE

Designer hopes to create a typeface that would take time to read since we consume massive amount of images on social media every day. The new typeface features a sharply contrasting curves mixed with at least one 90-degree angle for each character.

TD: Loris Pernoux

Fanny Ollas

Ceramics and Glass

Shut the door please!

When there is no place to go, when you need space. When you just need to breathe for a couple of minutes. When you need a place for reflection. When you need to hide. When you need to cry. When you need to swear to yourself in the mirror. When you need to say to yourself; I'm too good for this place…

The toilets are the only place in an office where you can shut the door and truly be by yourself; so please chose the one that fits your needs today.

Amanda Åkermo

Ädellab

"Joey"

In the late eighties, the planets are hovering in a certain pattern, somehow specifically beneficial to a Swedish satellite-suburb going under the name of Upplands Väsby. The local hockey-team manage to reach the first division and the Swedish king himself inaugurates the new hotel complex with its all glazed-in tower, reaching 70 meters and 24 floors above the Upplandic soil. The very name "Upplands Väsby" is losing ground to its famous epithet "Vilda Väsby" ("Wild Wäsby") and its true king is not Carl Gustav. About 26 kilometres further on in the same direction as the Infra city tower suggests hangs a glowing Constellation of stars called Europe. And the brightest star of them all, the burning supernova of Vilda Väsby is Joey.

Sabira Silcock

Ädellab

By manipulating small moments of connection and interaction between two bodies and the crafted object, the familiar experience of the smartphone notification is simulated, triggering emotional response. In reaction to the corporate environment, the playful nature of the piece winks at the frivolities of the "office party".

Dan-Fong Wang

Textiles

Finally, it rest in piece

Schrödinger's cat: The scenario presents a cat that may be simultaneously both alive and dead a state known as a quantum superposition, as a result of being linked to a random subatomic event that may or may not occur.

The time of image: a certain linear of time a time line with "start" and "end".

In this project, there are two certain time forms in a present: the time of installation, and the time of image/a dot and a line. Within the two different time form, similar to the theory, Schrödinger's cat, before the hand grenade explode, before we know the actual result, there are every possibility.

Lourdes González Osnaya

Textiles

Ausencia

The loss and the remains. An encounter with the absence in a room inhabited by silent traces of memories.

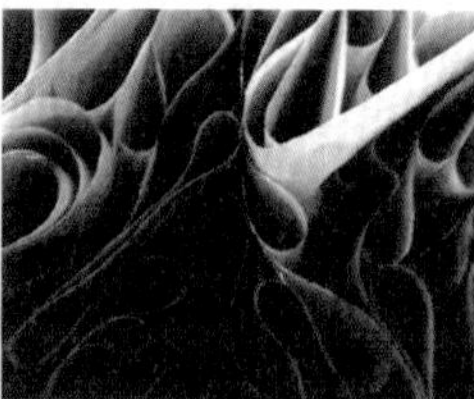

Marcelo Gustafsson

Ädellab

Membrane

Cytoplasmic membrane is a biological membrane which separates the interior cells from the outside world.

Bubbleplastic in itself is used as a membrane to keep objects safe during transportation.

Sofia Eriksson

Ädellab

A membrane is a selective barrier; letting some things pass through while it stops others. It could be the skin on your body, the walls of a building or an invisible barrier. It can be transformed or constructed by humans. The membrane is relating to its surrounding and is a passage between inside and outside, before and after.

Linda Ottosson

Ädellab

SKYMTA

We glimpse out, look past, look away. Pull down the blinds to later pull up. Turn the lights off and on. A clock is ticking as it always has and the newspaper is waiting in the letterbox. A constant flow of everyday repetitions that becomes unnoticed. But like cracks in a stream of permanence, so can the everyday become interrupted by interruptions and disorders, a knock on the door, a broken pot and a bruised elbow.

"Everything can become everyday, everything can become ordinary."
– Ben Highmore, *Ordinary Lives: Studies in the Everyday*

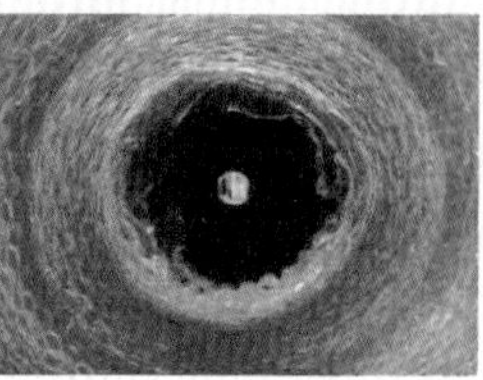

Alex Krissberg

Ceramics and Glass

Using traditional glass techniques mixed with invented techniques of my own, I create works which highlight the phenomenology of the making. In my work I focus on updating the tradition, but also referencing it. Along with this, I also want to make works that let others experience the craft of glass.

In the room I have made a large scale murrini (layered glass pulled and cut into slices) sketch which a person can walk inside of. In this way the viewer may experience how the space changes but also see how a murrini is built up out of layers.

Kristina Lundsjö

Textiles

KLG/self storage

I work with textiles that have been collected during many years. Piles of fabric that are just lying. They are loaded with dreams and expectations, waiting for something to be created.

In this project at Infracity, I have started in the other end, in the finished result: the frames. When framed, the work is finished.

I have made sketchy prototypes in cardboard out of my simple drawings. I present them in a separate meeting room where I have created an environment meant to feel like something between a storage and an art gallery.

Thanks to the sponsors:

LANGULAIRE

A B C D E F G H I J K L M
N O P Q R S T U V W X Y Z
0 1 2 3 4 5 6 7 8 9

¢ ¤ $ € £ ¥ ≈ ~ ÷ ∅ = > ≥ ∞ ∫
< ≤ ¬ − × ≠ ∂ % ‰ + ± ∏ √ ∑ Γ Δ Π Σ Ω
↑ ↗ → ↘ ↓ ↙ ← ↖ ↔ ↕
◊ ♡ | ¦ @ & ¶ © ® ℗ § ™ ° ℮ ℓ ^ † ‡

Inspired by the basic structures of hieroglyphics, graffiti, and calligraphy, the designer calls for a typeface that incorporates these combined features, so it has many features that seem to have met before. The designer creates deciphered pattern and uses suggestive skills to represent fonts in the form of illustrations. It challenges the perception of readers while arousing their imagination and curiosity for decoding the fonts.

Up to now, *Langulaire* has been widely used in books, visual advertising, exhibition poster, gallery sign, digital media, etc.

GRADUATION
SHOW
SCHOOL
OF
ARTS
ALL
THE
BEST
SINT-LUCAS GEN
ALEXIANENPLEIN 1
HOLSTRAAT DOMINICANE
25.6 2017
:00-18:00
24.06.17

TEN
TACU
LAR
#tentacularfestival
@mataderomadrid

JCDecaux

Festival de Tecnologías Críticas
y Aventuras Digitales

TENTACULAR

22 a 24 de noviembre 2018
tentacular.xyz

mataderomadrid.org

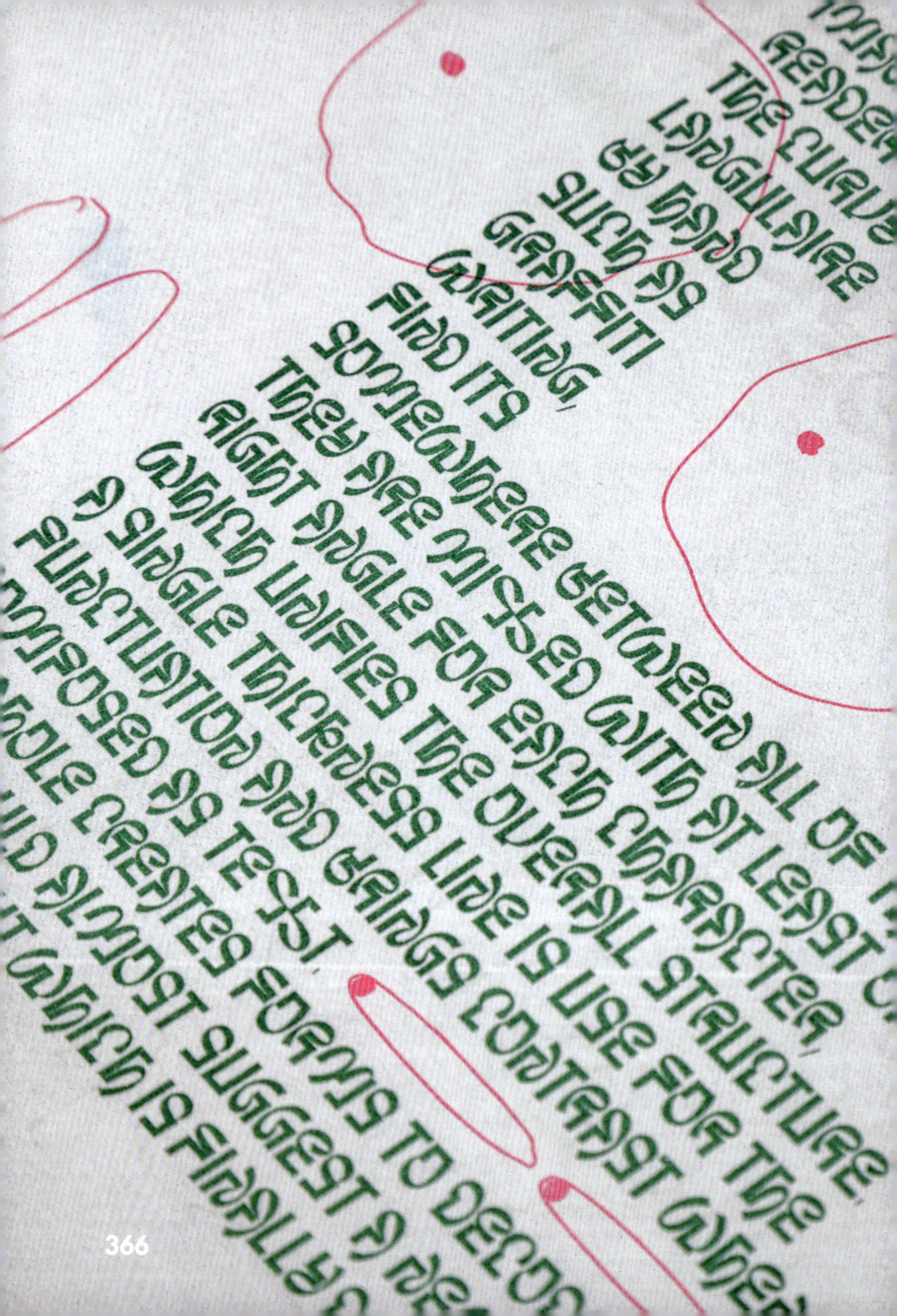

ACCELERATING POTENTIAL

Since the origins of mankind, transformations in the natural environment have been continuously present. Initially, men's relationship with nature was primarily limited to hunting, fishing and gathering. Later, significant changes were shaped by the discovery of fire, which has gradually led to transformations of forests into savannas and steppes.[1] Further evolutionary shift took place with the domestication of animals tamed for meat, milk and leather. Raising animals became a much more reliable food source compared to energy-consuming methods of hunter gatherers. However, the crucial turn in the relations between man and nature came with the Neolithic Revolution that introduced agriculture, which flourished at the beginning of the 10th millennium BC.

Cultivation of plants and animals catalyzed the process of population growth. From that time on, a chosen portion of the population provided steady food supplies for numerous social communities. World's first se lements began to accumulate around the agricultural fields which, with time, have transformed into progressive urban developments.[2]

At some point, this increasing density began to entail detrimental consequences. An example of systematic exploitation began in the ancient Middle East with the gradual clearing of cedar and cypress groves, which back then were the pride of Lebanon. Egyptian pharaohs and Assyrian or Babylonian kings used to build temples and palaces out of huge amounts of this valuable wood. Man's effort to domesticate and organize the land paved the way for the new era of humanity where nature was brought to the state of supreme productivity.

In the course of civilizational progress the belief in nature's inexhaustible resources began to form a collective mode of thinking which was reinforced with the beginnings of Industrial Revolution.

The 19th century of steam and electricity was one of intense human endeavor embodied in dynamically developing technological structures. These freshly born, profit-oriented systems triggered the continuous depredation of natural environment. It was not only a matter of further technical inventions designed for the cost-effective purposes intensifying production, but also the birth of a revelatory phenomenon which created the ongoing ethos of subduing the Earth.[3]

> "It expressed a new attitude to nature and to history. With ever-increasing zeal, scientific men and local worthies drawn from all classes explored the mineral wealth, the soils, the plant and animal life of each locality."[4]

These changes brought by the Industrial Revolution were acutely presented in the work of English cultural theorist, Francis Klingender, who analyzed different aesthetic shifts in literature as well as in painting, referring to the work of Gustav Doré, James McNeill Whistler or Jules Verne. New symbols of beauty sprouting on the plains of industrial landscape began to materialize in smoke-covered sceneries, sparking ironworks, smoking steam locomotives, bridges or dams. The industrial aesthetic reached its peak with the emergence of

ECONOMIC EXPANSIONISM

INFERIOR UTILITY

INCOME

UNCONSTRAINED ECONOMY

ANIMA MUNDI

Graphication Exaggeration

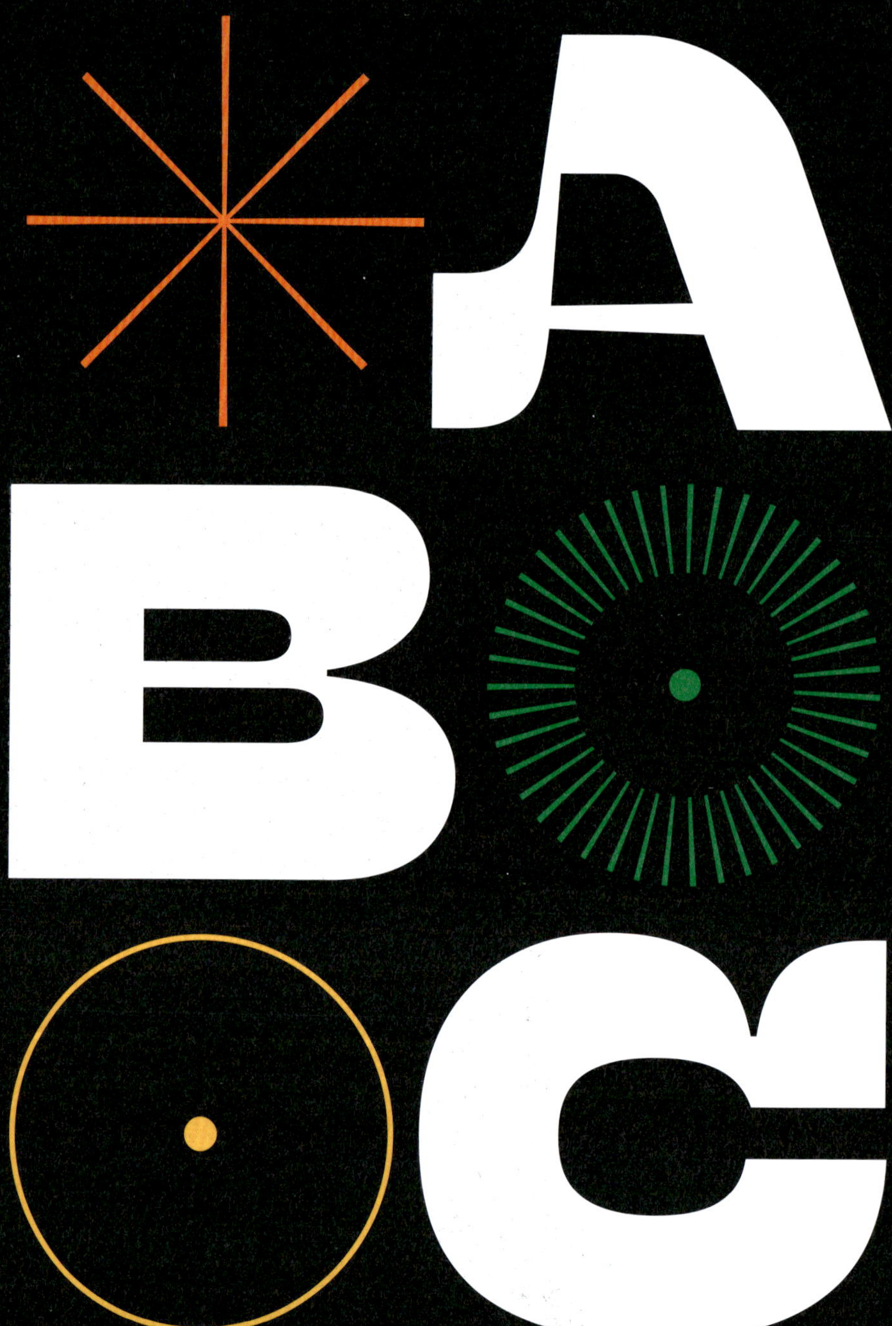

65. BURLE TYPE

Burle Marx Institute

Burle Marx Institute is an institution dedicated to the famous Brazilian architect and landscape designer Burle Marx. As one of the most influential artists in Brazil, his works are full of vibrancy and profoundly change the urban landscape. The design project invites the Brazilian design company Tátil to create the *Burle Type* as the visual subject for the Institute, aiming to reactivate, continue and expand the influence of Burle Marx as a cross-boundary aesthetic master. Its goal is to raise awareness for the importance of Roberto Burle Marx's contribution to the world and to echo the living art of his creative genius.

TD&D: Daniel Escudeiro
DA: Tátil Studio
CL: Burle Marx Institute

A A B C D E E F F G H I J K L

L M N O P Q R S T U V W X

Y Z 0 1 2 3 4 5 6 7 8 9 ! " # $

% & ' ( ) * + , - . / / : ; < = > ? @

[\ \ ] ^ _ ¯ { | } ~ € , ƒ „ … †

‡ ˆ ‰ ‹ › ' ' " " – — ○ ✳ ◎

⁄ ˜ ™ Œ ¡ ¢ £ ¤ ¥ ¦ § ¨ © ª

« ¬ ® ¯ ° ± ´ µ ¶ · º » - ¿ × ÷

Ç Đ Þ þ ß À Á Â Ã Ä Å Á

Â Ä À Å Ã Æ Ç È É Ê Ë É Ê

Ë È Ì Í Î Ï ð Ñ Ò Ó Ô Õ Ö Ø

Š Ù Ú Û Ü Ý Ÿ Ž 0 1 2 3 4

1/4 1/2 3/4 1/3 2/3 3/3 2/2 2/4 4/4

0 1 2 3 4 FI FL FFI FFL FL

FFL FLA FLA FZA FZA CA

ÇÃ CA ÇÃ KA KA LA LA QA

QA RA RA RX SS ZA ZA

One of the biggest challenges of the project is to create a unique visual symbol for a person with a strong personal style.

Burle Marx has an enduring influence on the later generations. To achieve the highest level of the design, the designer made extensive and in-depth research on his life, creation, and design philosophy, and then abstracted the highly visual elements to interpret the ideas and works of the master while arousing empathy and response. The final design of this robust and vivid customized typeface has left a key mark for continuing the precious aesthetic spirit.

INSTI
TUTO
BURLE
MARX

Roda de Conversa:

BURLE MARX:

LEGADO & CAMINHOS PARA O FUTURO.

INSTITUTO BURLE MARX

05.Nov
19h

Instituto
Moreira
Salles

www.
institutoburle
marx.org

KK MM

EE NN

236

66. FREN

This is an intriguing typeface. The designer reverses the inertial writing order and direction of the strokes based on the original. The deformation of each font is hard to grasp, but the overall readability is not affected.

TD: Dasha Levchuk

THERE ARE NOW ABOUT AS MANY DIFFERENT VARIETIES OF LETTERS AS THERE ARE DIFFERENT KINDS OF FOOLS

ERIC GILL

BEFORE
THE FALL

DIVERSITY IS A SIGN
OF LIFE AS IT IS
ACTUALLY LIVED

BRUNO
MUNARI

FORMS

ARE MODIFIIED DURING GROWTH BY THEIR SURROUNDINGS

TWO CONTINUOUS STRUCTURES MADE OF THE SAME NUMBER OF ELEMENTS CAN BE DIF-FERENT, ACCORDING TO THE TEMPERAMENTS OF WHOEVER ASSEMBLED THEM.

67. #USEDTOTHELIMIT - MAILING

The Studio designes this typeface in the spirit of environmental protection and recycling. Designers interpret sustainability in a new way: by making use of plastic waste. These seemingly useless materials are transformed into personalized greeting cards. The designers cut out transparent letters from the used plastic bags. Customers' initials are hand-printed on top of each other, the cards are made from recycled straws, and the words and seals are then hand-stamped.

D&TD: Maria Dierkes, Florian Loi
DA: EIGA Studio
CD: Henning Otto, Elisabeth Plass

Upcycled with love
from EIGA
#USEDTOTHELIMIT

Upcycled with love
— from EIGA
#USEDTOTHELIMIT

68. FUNKY EXPERIMENT ALPHABET

This is the typeface specially designed for the "36 Days of Type". The focus lies in keeping all the letters in tune without losing their uniqueness.

Designers create funny fonts by enlarging certain parts of them to make them more personal while maintaining the overall weight and making them recognizable at first glance.

TD: Nubia Navarro Aka Nubikini

69. RODA

This is a modular typeface with an air of authority. The vertical strokes are of even thickness, and the axe-shaped horizontal strokes create a sense of stability and certainty. It can be used for athletic materials that emphasize strength, as well as written messages including headings that desire attention.

TD: Dasha Levchuk

PROVE THEM WRONG

A MODULAR TYPEFACE IS AN ALPHABET CONSTRUCTED OUT OF A LIMITED NUMBER OF SHAPES OR MODULES

НА СТАРТ УВАГА РУШ

МОДУЛЬНІ ШРИФТИ - ЦЕ ШРИФТИ, ПОБУДОВАНІ НА ОСНОВІ ПРОСТИХ ГЕОМЕТРИЧНИХ ФОРМ

RODAFONT

RODA
8

국립극장 레퍼토리시즌
NATIONALREPERTORY
SEASON 2018–2019
7월 17일 티켓오픈
국립극장
국립극장
레퍼토리시즌
2018-2019

70. NTOK POSTER

The typeface is the main visual element of the poster for the National Repertory Season 2018-2019 of the National Theatre of Korea. The theatre has been running for 60 years and is a leading representative of the performing arts in Korea. Every season, the theatre would put on a variety of performances, such as stage plays, traditional plays, dances, and symphonies.

D: Jaemin Lee, Hyunsun You, Hyungwon Cho
DA: Studio fnt
CL: NTOK

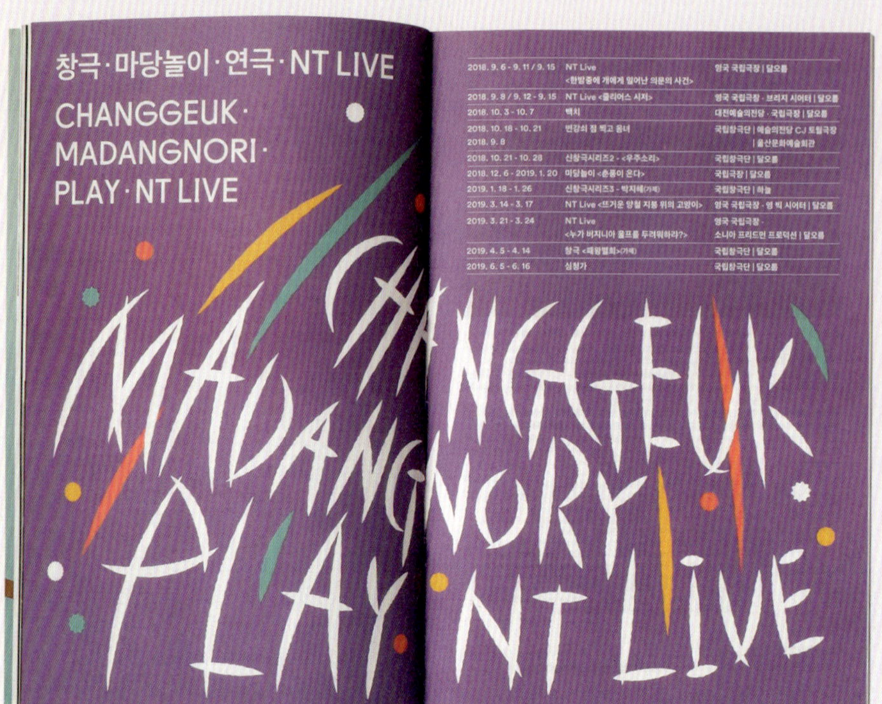
창극 · 마당놀이 · 연극 · NT LIVE
CHANGGEUK · MADANGNORI · PLAY · NT LIVE
2018. 9. 6 - 9. 11 / 9. 15 NT Live <한밤중에 개에게 일어난 의문의 사건> 영국 국립극장 | 달오름
2018. 9. 8 / 9. 12 - 9. 15 NT Live <줄리어스 시저> 영국 국립극장 · 브리지 시어터 | 달오름
2018. 10. 3 - 10. 7 백치 대전예술의전당 · 국립극장 | 달오름
2018. 10. 18 - 10. 21 변강쇠 점 찍고 옹녀 국립창극단 | 예술의전당 CJ 토월극장
2018. 9. 8 | 울산문화예술회관
2018. 10. 21 - 10. 28 신창극시리즈2 - <우주소리> 국립창극단 | 달오름
2018. 12. 6 - 2019. 1. 20 마당놀이 <춘풍이 온다> 국립극장 | 달오름
2019. 1. 18 - 1. 26 신창극시리즈3 - 박지혜(가제) 국립창극단 | 하늘
2019. 3. 14 - 3. 17 NT Live <뜨거운 양철 지붕 위의 고양이> 영국 국립극장 · 영 빅 시어터 | 달오름
2019. 3. 21 - 3. 24 NT Live <누가 버지니아 울프를 두려워하랴?> 영국 국립극장 · 소니아 프리드먼 프로덕션 | 달오름
2019. 4. 5 - 4. 14 창극 <패왕별희>(가제) 국립창극단 | 달오름
2019. 6. 5 - 6. 16 심청가 국립창극단 | 달오름
CHANGGEUK MADANGNORY PLAY NT LIVE

The art fonts on the posters is inspired from the shape of fireworks. Firework is one of the iconic elements of the NTOK, highlighting the strong festive atmosphere of the performance season. The designer uses four colors to draw the lines of fireworks, presenting a lively picture. The outline of the fonts made of the artistic and expressive lines symbolizes the bold and unrestrained fireworks and the artistic spirit of the theatre.

71. CAKO

Designed by Paris-based designer Jeremy Schneider, *Cako* is unique in its graphical glyphs and serifs, as well as its rich and stylized transformations, which give it a strong sense of rhythm. The typeface comes in three contrasting weights including black, regular, and very thin, which provide three different levels of impact. The contrast between weights is quite strong, together with elaborate details and spiky terminals.

TD: Jeremy Schneider
F: VJ Type

Cako

Raika

THE
SATURN
CIRCLE
&
THE FIRMAMENT

1234567

ÆŒæ

Jã

72. JAGER

Jager is a display typeface for heading or medium-length text. It took five years from the first sketch to the exhibition of contemporary crafts at the Musees des Arts Decoratifs in Paris.

Inspired by the superb crafts, the designer created the hollowed-out counter forms reminiscent of engravings, sculpture or working with chisels. The angles give the impression of having been cut in wood, the contours are rounded, never sharp in order to pay tribute to the delicate craftsman spirit.

TD: Jeremy Schneider
F: VJ Type

Jäger

Jogari
Motifs
Y. Klein
Figure

The design drew inspiration from the typography master Johann Michael Fleischmann. The sharp corners of the fonts look like cut wood, but they are rounded in outline with no sense of abruptness. The designer hopes to give it a sense of craftsmanship without nostalgia in designing the poster, which endows *Jager* with a distinctly modern aesthetic.There are two versions of each word weight. The original *Jager Master* has the boldest design, while *Jager Classic* offers another choice with a more rounded and varied silhouette.

Jacques-Laurent Agasse	JAGER	
1807		
Nine Greyhounds in a Landscape	Jager	Regular

Jager

Alphabet

Lowercases

Lowercases

abcdefg
hijklmno
pqrstuv
wxyz

Uppercases

ABCDEFG
HIJKLMNO
PQRSTUV
WXYZ

Figures

1234567890 ÆŒæœ

Index

References

[1] Aaron Betsky, Adrian Shaughnessy, Gert Staal,etc. New Perspectives in Typography[M]. Laurence King Publishing: London, 2015:30.

[2] Aaron Betsky, Adrian Shaughnessy, Gert Staal,etc.Thonik: Why We Design[M]. Lars Müller Publishers: Germany,2018:52.

[3] Chungyi Yeh . 字誌 01. [M]. FACES PUBLICATIONS, 2016.

[4] Chungyi Yeh . 字誌 03. [M]. FACES PUBLICATIONS, 2017.

[5] Harry Bennett.Stone lettering and variable fonts: What can the future of typography learn from the past?[EB/OL].https://www.itsnicethat.com/features/the-future-of-typography-graphic-design-290620,2020-06-29.

[6] Jyni Ong.Typeface Pickle-Standard both obeys and rejects the grid at the same time[EB/OL].https://www.itsnicethat.com/articles/benoit-bodhuin-pickles-standard-typeface-graphic-design-091118,2018-11-06.

[7] Neville Brody, Jon Wozencroft.FUSE 1-20[M].Taschen Press:Köln,2012:64.

[8] Scott Williams, Henrik Kubel.New Perspectives in Typography[M]. Laurence King Publishing:London,2015:30.

[9] Sendpoints 善本 . Typography Now-Design And Application Of Contemporary Typefaces[M]. Sendpoints, 2020:21.

[10] Steven Heller, Gail Anderson.The Typography Idea Book: Inspiration from 50 Masters (Type, Fonts, Graphic Design)[M]. Laurence King

[11] Steven Heller, Gail Anderson.Type Tells Tales[M].Thames & Hudson:London,2017:36.

[12] Toshi Omigari. Arcade Game Typography: The Art of Pixel Type[M].Thames & Hudson: London,2019:2.

[13] Thomas S. Mullaney.The Chinese Typewriter: A History[M]. The MIT Press: Cambridge,2017:64.

[14] Schmid H. Typography Today[M]. Bilingual edition. Japan:Seibundo Shinkosha, 2016.

RE-IMAGINE BIZARRE TYPE

First printing of the first edition, January 2022

sendpoints

PUBLISHED BY Sendpoints Publishing Co., Ltd.
ADDRESS: Unit 23, L1/F Mirror Tower, 61 Mody Road, Tsim Sha Tsui, Kowloon, Hong Kong, China
PUBLISHER: Lin Gengli
PUBLISHING DIRECTOR: Nicole Lo
CHIEF EDITOR: Nicole Lo
EXECUTIVE EDITOR: Wenyin Chen
DESIGN DIRECTOR: Dongyan Wu
EXECUTIVE ART EDITOR: Yanzi Lin
PROOFREADING: Wanting Zeng
TRANSLATOR: Xu Chao

SALES DIRECTOR: Philip Tsang
TEL: +852 6296 2246
EMAIL: sales@sppub.com
WEBSITE: www.sppub.com

ISBN 978-988-76087-4-5